The Rise of Universities

Foundations of Higher Education
Lionel S. Lewis, Series Editor

The Rise of
Universities

Charles Homer Haskins

with a new introduction by
Lionel S. Lewis

Transaction Publishers
New Brunswick (U.S.A.) and London (U.K.)

Library of Congress Catalog Number: 2001048078
ISBN: 0-7658-0895-1
Printed in the United States of America

Library of Congress Cataloging-in-Publication Data

Haskins, Charles Homer, 1870-1937.
    The rise of universities / Charles Homer Haskins ; with a new introduction by Lionel S. Lewis.
        p. cm.
    Originally published: New York : H. Holt and Co., 1923.
    Includes bibliographical references and index.
    ISBN 0-7658-0895-1 (alk. paper)
    1. Universities and colleges—History. 2. Education, Medieval. I. Title.

LA177 .H3 2001
378'.009—dc21   2001048078

TO MY STUDENTS
IN THREE UNIVERSITIES
1888–1923

CONTENTS

INTRODUCTION TO THE TRANSACTION EDITION
A COMPLEMENTARY ESSAY

CONTINUITY AND PARALLELS

THERE has not been a better analysis of "the ancient and universal company of scholars" than Charles Homer Haskins' *The Rise of Universities.* It is a superlative sketch of universities in Europe during their infancy in the Middle Ages, a flawless and effective distillation of what is known about their faculty, students, and curriculum. Eight decades after its publication it remains fresh and informative. It reminds us that the university—one of the great achievements of the Middle Ages, the period between the fall of Rome and the Italian Renaissance—has not only been a crucible fostering intellectual inquiry and creativ-

vii

ity, but continues after more than eight hundred years to be a primary center of teaching and learning around the world.

With his broad description of the mediaeval university, Haskins also helps us to understand a good deal more than what academic life was initially like. Indeed, from the opening paragraph, his exacting portrayal prompts us to remember how much more of our heritage—for example, the parliamentary process and trial by jury —is rooted in the Middle Ages.

The continuity of academic culture in universities since the very beginning has been truly remarkable. One cannot read Haskins without immediately seeing the influences of the mediaeval university on contemporary institutions of higher learning. Indeed, their broad outlines, from simple guilds of masters (teachers) and scholars (students) in the thirteenth century to the tangled multiversities of the twenty-first century, have hardly changed. Both the mediaeval and the modern university are centers of teaching and learning, particular places where teachers and students gather. Wherever located, this formalized structure for study and learning has a distinct culture, and this fact is recognized, sometimes grudgingly, by the larger community. It is this commonality, and the constancy of universities over centuries, that Haskins leads us to understand. It is striking how early institutional patterns have continued to shape the contemporary university despite great changes in knowledge and social life since the Middle Ages. Clearly, it is a marvel that the general form of the university has persisted for so long. Haskins' insightful volume moves us to understand why.

A NEW DEPARTURE

A confluence of factors made it possible for universities to begin to take shape in the Middle Ages. During the twelfth and thirteenth centuries, there was a substantial increase in the dissemination of Hellenic philosophy and science. In larger and larger numbers, translators were making available many

unknown or only partially known ancient texts and their commentaries. This
was the platform from which significant
intellectual advancement was launched.

Moreover, there were a number of influential teachers who attracted students from the ends of Europe, bringing
vitality to the particular locale where
they lectured, and creating the cultural
foundations from which university centers could grow. As a rule, one could set
up a school wherever one was able to find
sufficient students; a school's success or
failure largely depended on a teacher's
popularity and ability—and the students' willingness to pay fees. Like the
schools, as they began to evolve, universities were fluid, little more than a collection of teachers, each with his own
students.

The forceful presence of William of
Champeaux and the gifted logician Peter Abelard in Paris and of Pepo and
Irnerius in Bologna were the impetuses
of the intellectual movements that even-
tuated in the founding of the two archetypal centers of learning: the University

of Paris and the University of Bologna. The term "archetypal" is used because most aspects of the culture of the university, as it has been reproduced worldwide, can be traced back to one or the other. There are only a few fundamental features of other early universities—such as the University of Oxford, which advanced empirical studies—evident in contemporary universities.

Universities, as is the case with all institutions, developed to meet social needs. In the Middle Ages, it was becoming evident to leading churchmen that there was a need for theologians and lay intellectuals who would be able to reconcile the newly rediscovered classical ideas with Christian revelation. More importantly, there was a growing demand for individuals who had studied a subject in depth, who had specialized knowledge not only of theology, but of canon law, of civil law, or of medicine, to teach these subjects to a growing number of practitioners.

In monasteries and, more so, the cathedral schools in places like Chartres,

Laon, Liège, Orléans, Paris, Rheims, Rouen, and Utrecht, organized curricula evolved that went beyond the basics of these subjects; yet these schools did not promote higher learning. Centers of higher learning to educate those who wished to teach, master, and apply the most advanced elements of learning were required. These embryonic centers—in Bologna for the study of law and in Paris for the study of logic, philosophy, and theology—were to become the first universities. As the most vital seats of study and learning, over time, monastic schools were replaced by cathedral schools, out of which would develop universities. From Bologna and Paris, the university movement spread across Europe in all directions, to Austria, Germany, Hungary, Poland, Portugal, Spain, and Scotland.

Contrary to what is sometimes believed, idle curiosity was not a vital force in the nascent university. More important to the revival of learning and the growth of universities was the education of professionals who could pursue religious, governmental, administrative, or legal careers. The need to enlarge professional education was rooted in and consistent with the very utilitarian theme of Roman education, by which schools were primarily used to train and recruit imperial officials, and which was guided by the belief that those with the most knowledge were prepared to be the most effective leaders.

Thus, it could not be said that humanistic learning, the study of language and literature, was a principal factor in the university's development. In fact, this was mostly neglected until the Renaissance. It is true that many works of classical learning and literature which had found their way to Western Europe, although not necessarily taught, were sheltered in monasteries during early mediaeval times. In surviving the Norse invasions in France and elsewhere in the eighth to tenth centuries, monasteries were able to protect and save their books and manuscripts, and therefore were instrumental in preserving a good deal of what centuries later is important to the culture of learning.

THE RISE OF UNIVERSITIES

There are few historical accounts that record the birth of the university. The statutes from the University of Cambridge from between 1236 and 1254 are the earliest reliable texts that have been preserved. However, there are documents from the University of Paris that date from between 1200 and 1215: a charter of Philip Augustus; statutes passed by the masters, along with their formal recognition as a corporate body by Pope Innocent III; and rules dealing with academic dress, funerals, and "the accustomed order in lectures and disputations." There is no way of telling how long before this time universities had been in existence. (A claim from the University of Bologna dates it from 1088, although the first direct evidence of its existence is from a statement by Boncompagno in 1215. Using documents, the founding of the University of Paris can be set with some reliability at 1208.) We only know that the contours of universities slowly took shape; they had become a fact well before being given a name.

Schools, as institutions, particularly those for religious training, existed in Western Europe and elsewhere long before the Middle Ages, as had academies of higher learning such as the philosophical schools of Athens dating from the fourth century B.C. Historians have described in detail early Islamic and Chinese higher education. However, there is no evidence that there had been formalized, structured organizations created for the express purpose of educating individuals in particular disciplines that were not part of a religious body. Universities were created to be separate, secular, independent institutions. However, given that a large proportion of their students were clerics, and given the considerable power of popes, emperors, and kings, they were from the beginning, of course, somewhat less than this.

The Church had much to do with who taught and what was taught. In 1215, a cardinal legate set forth the following rules for the University of Paris:

> No one shall lecture in the arts at Paris before he is twenty-one years of age, and

he shall have heard lectures for at least six years before he begins to lecture, and he shall promise to lecture for at least two years.... He shall not be stained by any infamy, and when he is ready to lecture, he shall be examined according to the form which is contained in the writing of the lord bishop of Paris, where is contained the peace confirmed between the chancellor and scholars by judges delegated by the pope.... And they shall lecture on the books of Aristotle on dialectic old and new in the schools ordinarily and not *ad cursum* [the extraordinary or afternoon lectures]. They shall also lecture on both Priscians ordinarily, or at least on one. They shall not lecture on feast days except on philosophers and rhetoric and the *quadrivium*.... They shall not lecture on the books of Aristotle on metaphysics and natural philosophy or on summaries of them...

Religion was clearly the most pervasive inspiration in the life and work of the university. It goes without saying that no one was free to teach atheism or heresy.

Colleges came into being after universities. Originally they were not institutions of education, but in Paris endowed residences or hostels for students. In Bologna, they were rooted in the organized guilds of masters. Some eventually did institute a course of study, although they were not, and still are not, as all-encompassing as universities. As they matured, they became autonomous, self-governing, legal entities, with their own statutes and privileges. In Paris and generally in France, the university assumed control over the college; English colleges, for the most part, developed independently from university authorities. That contemporary colleges may stand alone or be part of a university continues to be confusing to some.

GUILDS AND THEIR PRIVILEGES

The inchoate university was the institutionalization of guilds of masters and scholars that was much like the European guilds of merchants, craftsmen, artisans, or mechanics in the twelfth century. These associations or corporations were organized for those with a common interest or calling to gain advantage over other collectivities. Indeed, the term *universitas* simply means "the whole" and was used in reference to guilds. It is found in Cicero referring to the whole of mankind. By the Middle Ages, it designated a group having juridical existence.

What was at first a general term to denote an aggregate (or collectivity or body), was by the early 1220s adopted as a shorthand label applied to those—teachers and students (*universitas magistrorum et scholarium*)—involved in higher learning, heretofore referred to as a *studium generale*, that is, a place attracting scholars from all parts.

Much as a trade guild trained an apprentice to become a journeyman and then a master craftsman, the mediaeval student took instruction for his degree of master of arts or doctor of law or medicine, after which he was free to follow his trade, which was to lecture, to be a professor. It may be said that the tools in a university were books and manuscripts and that those who taught were trading in knowledge much the way artisans sold their wares.

Generally, mediaevalists agree, the university as an independent, legal corporation first appeared in the early decades of the thirteenth century. The formal recognition of a body of individuals who were engaged in teaching and learning made universities a reality. This fact of organization formally separated those within a university from those without. Universities became institutions standing on their own. As recognized entities, they had the autonomy of any corporate body.

The associations of masters and scholars were able to organize prescribed courses of study and faculties, establish a system of degree requirements and examinations, and set responsibilities and privileges. The body of norms that grew around teaching and learning became the model for all subsequent universities, some evolving slowly and others taking shape immediately after a migration of masters and scholars. Later, universities were established through the initiatives of civil or ecclesiastical authorities for spiritual or temporal reasons—piety, prestige, ambition, or economic gain.

Originally a degree was nothing more than a license to teach (*licentia docendi*) or the right given to a university to grant a graduate a license to teach anywhere without further examination (*ius ubique docendi*)—a union card, as the degree is sometimes dismissively referred to today. In fact, in French the term for degree is still *licence* and for a graduate it is *licencié*.

In short, the genesis of the mediaeval university was individuals with a common interest in a subject or in a teacher, who were attracted to a place, and who, over time, organized. Many were foreigners and, for support and safety, it was especially necessary to affiliate. Eventually, graduation came to mean more than simply admission into the society of teachers, but became a definite legal status. University faculty began to see their status as being something special, and this view was generally shared by the wider society, including its civic and religious leaders.

A decree in 1158 granting students in Bologna special ecclesiastical jurisdiction was issued by Frederick I. This was, in effect, a de facto acknowledgment that they by themselves could be a corporate body. (It also, importantly, served to encourage students not to migrate to other domains.) Only forty-two years later, to the north, the king of France issued a similar charter, this one to palliate an outbreak of violence which began after a quarrel between the servant of a German scholar and an innkeeper. The civil and church rulings which were to follow—for example, one regarding the setting of rents for masters and scholars—imply the existence of norms and customs and associations and formal groupings, all elements of institutions.

With wondrous regularity, popes and emperors—in the Roman tradition of rescripts—commanded civil authorities to grant an array of dispensations (rights, liberties, and immunities) to masters and scholars, all serving to set off the university from the larger society. Two important and common exemptions were from taxation and military service. Masters and scholars were often also placed under the protection of special courts. All of these actions were the basis for the growing independence of the young and economically fragile university.

Without buildings, a campus, or much in the way of accouterments, the university—the community of teachers and students—was free to pack up and leave a locality if for some reason they felt mistreated and unhappy. They could, and did, use the threat of departure to extract indulgences from authorities who were loath to have them abandon a location. Some of the prerogatives they derived are at the base of what centuries later have become principles of academic freedom. As the following brief excerpt shows, even a pope would go to considerable lengths to placate faculty and students who believed themselves wronged:

But since the masters and the scholars who suffered injury and damage from the breaking of the oath made to them by the city of Paris have departed from the university, they seem to have pled not so much their own case as the common cause. We, with the general need and utility of the Church in view, will and order that henceforth the privileges shall be shown to the masters and scholars by our dearest son of Christ, the illustrious king of France, and fines inflicted on their malefactors, so that they may lawfully study at Paris without any further delay or return of infamy or irregularity of notation. To no man then be it licit to infringe or with rash daring to contradict this page of our provision, constitution, and inhibition. If anyone shall presume to attempt this, let him know that he will incur the wrath of almighty God and of the blessed apostles Peter and Paul.

This particular bull was sufficient to induce the university to return to the city after having abruptly abandoned it nearly two years earlier. Paris was a city of teachers and students. One estimate was that students comprised ten percent of its population, too large and important a number economically to lose in the event that the university permanently settled elsewhere.

From the beginning, students especially have had to be placated so that they would not move elsewhere. The University of Cambridge began in 1209, when a number of disaffected students moved there from the University of Oxford. Twenty years later, Oxford as well benefited from a migration of students from Paris.

In essence, it was students who organized the University of Bologna (and other Italian universities). They ran it, hired and imposed discipline on faculty, and elected the administrative staff. It had originally been started as a university of masters, but the older and wealthier students quickly gained the upper hand and were able to establish detailed regulations. Until the end of the eighteenth century, after Napoleon had captured the city, the rector was a student, although before then, those who taught, since they held the right to examine and issue certificates to teach, maintained a considerable degree of power over academic affairs. Perhaps because of this history, Bologna's curriculum was decidedly utilitarian, focusing almost completely on preparing students for career advancement.

For the most part, the contemporary university has been shaped from those institutions where masters banded together for mutual protection—commonly referred to as the Paris model—and not those built around groups of organized scholars—the Bologna model. In the effort to prevent the spread of student-controlled universities, the still-heard argument was advanced that by themselves students did not compose a class; they were simply "pupils of the doctors of the law." Faculty currently and universally regulate instruction and other university affairs more so than do students.

A dominant theme in the rise of universities was the constant struggle for autonomy. In some sense, contemporary faculty have less autonomy than did the masters of mediaeval universities, who pretty much controlled institutional affairs, both academic and nonacademic. There was no governing board (regents were all of those who actually engaged in teaching), administrative hierarchy, or body of wealthy benefactors to interfere or impose its will on the direction of study. There was only the Church, to be sure, a not inconsiderable force. After princes and communities began providing financial support, considerable independence, and eventually privileges—for example, how teaching appointments were determined—were permanently lost.

In the roughly 350-year period from the late twelfth to the early sixteenth centuries, between six and seven dozen universities were founded in Europe. Most were first housed in private residences, rented space, or church property. As they grew, they acquired their own collection of buildings and land. This reduced their independence by greatly diminishing the ability to move when aggrieved. Eventually, they became self-contained campuses, what many—academics and non-academics alike—today mistakenly conclude is the sine qua non of a university.

THE UNIVERSITY CURRICULUM

As they began to emerge, some attention was paid to the body of literature which became known as Christian humanism, but the heart of the mediaeval university's curriculum came from the ancient Greeks through the Romans. Boethius' scientific treatises on astronomy, rhetoric, logic, arithmetic, and music and his translations from Greek to Latin were a significant source of information on a wide variety of topics.

The most studied and influential thinker throughout the Middle Ages was Aristotle; by 1200, Boethius' translations of his work had become central to the philosophy curriculum in Paris, which was steadily spreading to other institutions. For three hundred years, until the sixteenth century, Aristotelianism pretty much dominated studies in the faculty of arts, what would now be called the liberal arts. Particularly important to university scholarship from the Middle Ages almost uninterruptedly onward was one of its central ideas: that knowledge could be ordered and its truths rationally tested. The dissemination of the corpus of Aristotelian writings in translations of varying accuracy contributed materially to the rise of the university; of somewhat lesser importance was a renewed interest in Roman and ecclesiastical law and the greater availability of pre-existent medical and scientific books and manuscripts.

At first, Aristotle's writing was known chiefly through his treatises on logic, which set the standards for rational analysis. This work, the *Organon* (principles for scientific or philosophical investigation), offered a detailed treatment of the syllogism and an analysis of proof. As his *Physics* and other writings on natural philosophy (e.g., theories of the universe, of motion and of time and place, and discussions of psychology, which were translated partly from Arabic and partly directly from Greek) gained prominence, he was accepted as the pre-eminent authority on almost all philosophical and scientific inquiry. Scholasticism, which was rooted in the authority of both the Catholic Church and Aristotle and his commentators, became the dominant intellectual current of mediaeval universities. This union of faith and reason represented a conservative intellectual style, not one of innovation.

The curriculum, even so, was far from being all Aristotelian. The logic of Porphyry, a noted commentator on Aristotle, and Gilbert de la Porrée were also standard. Adelard of Bath's translation of an Arabic version of Euclid's *Elements* became a standard mathematics textbook for centuries. The Latin grammars of Priscian (notably his *Institutiones Grammaticae*) and Donatus were widely used, as was Ptolemy's work on astronomy. Cicero was used for the study of rhetoric.

Besides teaching and learning in the *artes* (often called arts and sciences or philosophy), the complete mediaeval university had, as an ideal, instruction in medicine, theology, and law. When the University of Prague was founded by Charles IV in 1348, it was designed to have four faculties, divided along these lines. Again, four decades later, the original charter of the University of Heidelberg decreed that it "shall be ruled, disposed, and regulated according to the modes and matters accustomed to be observed in the University of Paris.... [T]he latter's steps shall be imitated in every way possible; so that, namely, there shall be four faculties in it..."

Notwithstanding the fact that the principal texts for the study of medicine were by the Greek physicians Hippocrates and Galen (as well as the Persian Avicenna), the ideas of the Greeks were a little less central in the more applied areas of the curriculum. The focus of theological studies was the Bible and Peter Lombard's *Sentences*, which, in codifying and clarifying the sacraments, became the standard text and the starting point of all doctrinal study and controversy throughout the Middle Ages.

It appears that from the earliest days, more students in mediaeval universities studied law than any other advanced subject. Typically, law faculties were divided into Roman Civil Law, as brought together in the sixth century under the direction of the Emperor Justinian I, and Canon Law. At Bologna, Irnerius (1055/60-1125) introduced the study of Roman Law. With an eye toward establishing principles of justice, he began with the Justinian codes; going beyond simply adapting them, he added extensive explanations to the text with notes, parallel passages, and glosses. By the fourteenth century, this curriculum had spread to other centers of learning.

In his *Decretum*, Gratian, who also taught at Bologna, codified Canon Law—rules relating to faith, morals, and discipline which had evolved over the centuries—by compiling and systematizing the imperatives of Catholicism from various councils, synods, decrees, and the extensive letters of the popes. In setting forth the opinions of so many others as well as his own, in reconciling the apparent contradictions of Canon Law and making it more consistent, his great work was as much a service to the Church as a scholarly achievement. Once again, it is apparent from the curriculum that interpretation and transmission of knowledge, not its advancement through investigation or learning for its own sake, were the major intellectual currents that first shaped the mediaeval university.

It was believed that the starting point of education, and of the way to wisdom, until the end of the eighteenth century, was the seven liberal arts, divided into the *trivium* and the *quadrivium*, three verbal and four mathematical disciplines. The former consisted of instruction in grammar (Latin grammar, mastering its rules, and improving reading and writing), rhetoric (the arts of both public speaking and letter writing), and dialectic (polishing reasoning and debating skills). The latter consisted of arithmetic (an introduction to the significance of numbers and simple calculation), geometry (geography, surveying, and the ability to measure planes and lines), astronomy (the study of stars and their annual course), and music (a theoretical and mathematical approach). On the whole, the curriculum was in direct descent from Greek philosophy. By the twelfth century, the university curriculum consisted of these seven liberal arts, but also of what was called the new logic and the new mathematics, as well as the advanced courses in law, medicine, and theology. Long after Roger Bacon argued that university instruction should encompass natural science, observation, and experimentation were still largely marginal to university study.

The *trivium* and *quadrivium* were seen as the basic and best instruments to prepare the mind to continue to learn. Few questioned the assumption that their elements were the foundations of knowledge, able to reveal pure and simple truths. They could explain other things;

other things could not explain them. One's basic formal education was considered complete after the seven were mastered.

As is often the case, those in control of universities and their curricula saw special and considerable value in what was taught and how it was taught. They ardently believed that knowledge had reached its zenith, and that the traditional course of study need only be followed; indeed, they were convinced that there were great risks in doing otherwise. One example of the defense of tradition and an assault on the new and different can be seen in a letter from the Bishop of Tournai to the pope, written between the last decade of the twelfth century and the first decade of the thirteenth century:

> The studies of sacred letters among us are fallen into the workshop of confusion, while both disciples applaud novelties alone and masters watch out for glory rather than learning. They everywhere compose new and recent *summulae* and commentaries, by which they attract, de-

tain, and deceive their hearers....
[F]aculties called liberal [free] having lost
their pristine liberty are sunk in such
servitude that adolescents with long hair
impudently usurp their professorships,
and beardless youths sit in the seat of
their seniors, and those who don't yet
know how to be disciples strive to be
named masters. And they write their
summulae moistened with drool and
dribble but unseasoned with the salt of
philosophers. Omitting the rules of the
arts and discarding the authentic books
of the artificers, they seize the flies of
empty words in their sophisms like the
claws of spiders. Philosophy cries that
her garments are torn and disordered...

One cannot help being struck by the contemporary ring of this lament.

Contrary to what is often assumed, the
seven subjects of the liberal arts were
not nearly equally emphasized. At those
universities, like the University of Paris,
with a special interest in philosophical
and theological matters, the dialectic
was at the center of the curriculum—
"the science of science." On the other
hand, at those Italian universities where

the study of law took precedence, where public speaking and persuasion were basic tools for graduates who would effectively serve the Church or state, more time was given to grammar and rhetoric. With the syllogism being central to disputation, classical learning had little chance of gaining a foothold, regardless of trenchant criticism from some quarters. The scholar, humanist, and churchman John of Salisbury (secretary to Thomas Becket and bishop of Chartres), for one, wrote: "That just as dialectic facilitates other disciplines, so, if studied alone, it remains lifeless and sterile, nor does it stimulate the soul to bear fruits of philosophy, unless it conceives elsewhere." As Haskins notes in his *The Renaissance of the Twelfth Century,* first published four years after *The Rise of Universities*:

> Yet, in point of fact, it was not religion but logic and practical interests that proved the most dangerous enemies of the classics and finally killed the classical renaissance of the twelfth century. The reception of Aristotle's *New Logic* toward the middle of the century threw a heavy

weight on the side of dialectic in the balance of the liberal arts, and the disparity grew with the further recovery of the Aristotelian *corpus*. With so much logic and philosophy to master, there is little time and less inclination for the leisurely study of letters. Logic is in the saddle, and literature must give way.

There were few ways and means of instruction; lectures to comment on and interpret course readings, repetition, disputations conducted according to the rules of Aristotelian syllogistics, conferences, quizzes, and examinations were all used to enhance learning. One significant but often overlooked innovation of the mediaeval university was to link teaching and examinations closely together.

In part, because there was only a limited amount of reading material available, there were a limited number of books with which students were expected to become familiar. Basic instruction in the arts lasted about six years, between the ages of fourteen and twenty. The bachelor's degree simply marked the end of the first stage of higher learning, and certified the capacity and right to teach under supervision. To earn a master's privileges required another three, four, or even more years of study beyond the *baccalaureate*.

The educational theory that guided students was straightforward: it was expected that they understand and retain what was taught. Much like students throughout the ages, they were constantly pressed to study assiduously. Most who were unsuccessful failed because of ill health or inadequate funds or the inability to master memorization or the joining of learning and morals. An official of the Curia in Avignon found many reasons to explain the downfall of students.

1. Sometimes they wish to be above their masters, impugning their statements more with a certain wrongheadedness than with reason....

3. They attend classes but make no effort to learn anything....

4. They frequently learn what they would better ignore....

5. On obscure points, they depend on their own judgment.... For they are

ashamed to ask of others what they themselves don't know, which is stupid pride...

7. They have among themselves evil and disgraceful societies, associating together for ill...

8. They are disobedient...

9. On feast days they don't go to church...but gad about town.... Or, if they go to church, it is not for worship, but to see girls or swap stories.

10. They foment rows...

12. The expense money which they have from their parents or churches they spend in taverns, conviviality, games, and other superfluities, and they return home empty, without knowledge, conscience, or money....

13. They contract debts...

Plus ça change, plus c'est la même chose.

All instruction in universities was given in Latin; in this sense, universities transcended states and regional culture. They were not local or even national, and were a good deal alike. The common curriculum for students from the Iberian Peninsula to the British Isles and countries to the east and in between resulted at least minimally in homogenizing the culture of Western Europe. It surely worked to weaken provincialism. To the extent that a degree granted equal privileges and opportunities to all recipients, it—along with birth and wealth— became a means of access to prominence and power. Higher education made social mobility possible for some of peasant birth, thus helping to loosen the rigid class lines of feudalism. The university worked to make achievement more important, ascription less so. It became an instrument for social mobility; at the University of Vienna between 1377 and 1413, twenty-five percent of the students made the claim that they were poor (although the actual number may not have been quite as large). It has continued to have a democratizing effect on the larger social structure.

Although not all faculty in a discipline taught the same material and not all students in a discipline were expected to read and study the same books and manuscripts, it could pretty much be guessed

xl

the amount of learning a degree in a discipline represented. This is much less true today; in most disciplines, particularly non-scientific ones, the variation in what students may have learned is now considerably greater. Given the wide range of experiences of the contemporary student and the greater span of knowledge, the argument for a return of the often revered Western Canon (so that at least undergraduates might have some sense of their cultural heritage), much discussed by serious thinkers in the United States in the later decades of the twentieth century, seems futile. The success of the even more modest goal of providing a minimum liberal arts education to students in order to enrich their lives has, at best, been mixed.

CHARLES HOMER HASKINS

Charles Homer Haskins (1870-1937) received his B.A. in 1887 and his Ph.D. in 1890 from the Johns Hopkins University. After teaching at the University of Wisconsin for a decade, he spent the remainder of his academic career at Harvard University, first as the Gurney Professor of History and Political Science and then as the Henry Charles Lea Professor of Mediaeval History. He also served as the dean of the Graduate School of Arts and Sciences from 1908 until 1924. Outside of academia, he served as a member of the Peace Commission after World War I.

Among his many publications are *Norman Institutions* (1918), *Studies in the History of Mediaeval Science* (1924), and *Studies in Mediaeval Culture* (1929).

At the time of his death, it was said that *The Rise of Universities*, originally the Colver Lectures delivered at Brown University in 1923, was one of his books through which "he accomplished the nobler, and the harder, task of scholarship—the conversion of science into art."

Lionel S. Lewis

TRANSACTION INTRODUCTION

SUPPLEMENTAL READINGS

The following brief list of books is a useful complement to *The Rise of Universities*:

Charles Homer Haskins, *The Renaissance of the Twelfth Century*, Cambridge: Harvard University Press, 1927.

Ernest F. Henderson, *Select Historical Documents of the Middle Ages*, London: George Bell and Sons, 1892. (Reprinted: New York: AMS Press, 1968.)

Arthur O. Norton, *Readings in the History of Education: Mediaeval Universities*, Cambridge: Harvard University Press, 1909.

Hastings Rashdall, *The Universities of Europe in the Middle Ages*, (Volume I and Volume II [Parts I and II]), Oxford: Oxford University Press, 1895.

Lynn Thorndike, *University Records and Life in the Middle Ages*, New York: Columbia University Press, 1944.

Helene Wieruszowski, *The Medieval University: Masters, Students, Learning*, Princeton: D. Van Nostrand, 1966.

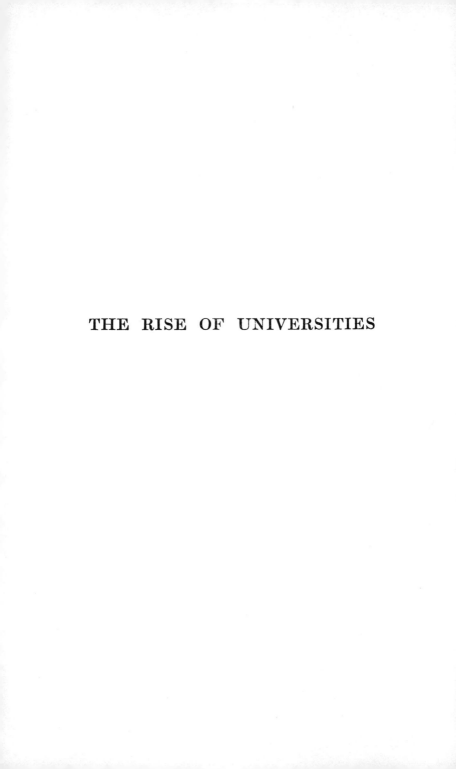

THE RISE OF UNIVERSITIES

THE
RISE OF UNIVERSITIES

I

THE EARLIEST UNIVERSITIES

UNIVERSITIES, like cathedrals and parliaments, are a product of the Middle Ages. The Greeks and the Romans, strange as it may seem, had no universities in the sense in which the word has been used for the past seven or eight centuries. They had higher education, but the terms are not synonymous. Much of their instruction in law, rhetoric, and philosophy it would be hard to surpass, but it was not organized into the form of permanent institutions of learning. A great teacher like Socrates gave no diplomas; if a modern student sat at his feet for three months, he would demand a certificate, something tangible and external to show for it — an excellent theme, by the way, for a Socratic dialogue. Only in the twelfth and thirteenth centuries do there emerge in the world those features of organized education with which we are most familiar, all that machinery of instruction represented by faculties and colleges and courses of study, examinations and commencements and academic degrees. In all these matters we are the heirs and successors, not of Athens and Alexandria, but of Paris and Bologna.

The contrast between these earliest universities and those of today is of course broad and striking. Throughout the period of its origins the mediaeval university had no libraries, laboratories, or museums, no endowment or buildings of its own; it could not possibly have met the requirements of the Carnegie Foundation! As an historical text-book from one of the youngest of American universities tells us, with an unconscious touch of local color, it had " none of the attributes of the material existence which with us are so self-evident." The mediaeval university was, in the fine old phrase of Pasquier, " built of men " — *bâtie en hommes*. Such a university had no board of trustees and published no catalogue; it had no student societies — except so far as the university itself was fundamentally a society of students — no college journalism, no dramatics, no athletics, none of those " outside activities " which are the chief excuse for inside inactivity in the American college.

And yet, great as these differences are, the fact remains that the university of the twentieth century is the lineal descendant of mediaeval Paris and Bologna. They are the rock whence we were hewn, the hole of the pit whence we were digged. The fundamental organization is the same, the historic continuity is unbroken. They created the university tradition of the modern world, that common tradition which belongs to all our institutions of higher learning, the newest as well as the oldest, and which all college and university men should know and cherish. The origin and nature of these earliest universities is the subject of these three lectures. The first will deal with university institutions, the second with university instruction, the third with the life of university students.

In recent years the early history of universities has begun to attract the serious attention of historical scholars, and mediaeval institutions of learning have at last been lifted out of the region of myth and fable where they long lay obscured. We now know that the foundation of the University of Oxford was not one of the many virtues which the millennial celebration could properly ascribe to King Alfred; that Bologna did not go back to the Emperor Theodosius; that the University of Paris did not exist in the time of Charlemagne, or for nearly four centuries afterward. It is hard, even for the modern world, to realize that many things had no founder or fixed date of beginning but instead " just grew," arising slowly and silently without definite record. This explains why, in spite of all the researches of Father Denifle and Dean Rashdall and the local antiquaries, the beginnings of the oldest universities are obscure and often uncertain, so that we must content ourselves sometimes with very general statements.

The occasion for the rise of universities was a great revival of learning, not that revival of the fourteenth and fifteenth centuries to which the term is usually applied, but an earlier revival, less known though in its way quite as significant, which historians now call the renaissance of the twelfth century. So long as knowledge was limited to the seven liberal arts of the early Middle Ages, there could be no universities, for there was nothing to teach beyond the bare elements of grammar, rhetoric, logic, and the still barer notions of arithmetic, astronomy, geometry, and music, which did duty for an academic curriculum. Between 1100 and 1200, however, there came a great influx of new knowledge into western Europe, partly through Italy and Sicily, but chiefly through the Arab scholars of Spain — the works of Aristotle, Euclid, Ptolemy, and the Greek physicians, the new arithmetic, and those texts of the Roman law which had lain hidden through the Dark Ages. In addition to the elementary propositions of triangle and circle, Europe now had those books of plane and solid geometry which have done duty in schools and colleges ever since; instead of the painful operations with Roman numerals — how painful one can readily see by trying a simple problem of multiplication or division with these characters — it was now possible to work readily with Arabic figures; in the place of Boethius the " Master of them that know " became the teacher of Europe in logic, metaphysics, and ethics. In law and medicine men now possessed the fulness of ancient learning. This new knowledge burst the bonds of the cathedral and monastery schools and created the learned professions; it drew over mountains and across the narrow seas eager youths who, like Chaucer's Oxford clerk of a later day, 'would gladly learn and gladly teach,' to form in Paris and Bologna those academic gilds which have given us our first and our best definition of a university, a society of masters and scholars.

To this general statement concerning the twelfth century there is one partial exception, the medical university of Salerno. Here, a day's journey to the south of Naples, in territory at first Lombard and later Norman, but still in close contact with the Greek East, a school of medicine had existed as early as the middle of the eleventh century, and for perhaps two hundred years thereafter it was the most renowned medical centre in Europe. In this " city of Hippocrates " the medical writings of the ancient Greeks were expounded and even developed on the side of anatomy and surgery, while its teachings were condensed into pithy maxims of hygiene which have not yet lost their vogue — "after dinner walk a mile," etc. Of the academic organization of Salerno we know nothing before 1231, and when in this year the standardizing hand of Frederick II regulated its degrees Salerno had already been distanced by newer universities farther north. Important in the history of medicine, it had no influence on the growth of university institutions.

If the University of Salerno is older in time, that of Bologna has a much larger place in the development of higher education. And while Salerno was known only as a school of medicine, Bologna was a many-sided institution, though most noteworthy as the centre of the revival of the Roman law. Contrary to a common impression, the Roman law did not disappear from the West in the early Middle Ages, but its influence was greatly diminished as a result of the Germanic invasions. Side by side with the Germanic

jejune – void of interest; lacking nutritive value

codes, Roman law survived as the customary law of the Roman population, known no longer through the great law books of Justinian but in elementary manuals and form-books which grew thinner and more jejune as time went on. The *Digest,* the most important part of the *Corpus Juris Civilis,* disappears from view between 603 and 1076; only two manuscripts survived; in Maitland's phrase, it " barely escaped with its life." Legal study persisted, if at all, merely as an apprenticeship in the drafting of documents, a form of applied rhetoric. Then, late in the eleventh century, and closely connected with the revival of trade and town life, came a revival of law, foreshadowing the renaissance of the century which followed. This revival can be traced at more than one point in Italy, perhaps not first at Bologna, but here it soon found its centre for the geographical reasons which, then as now, made this city the meeting-point of the chief routes of communication in northern Italy.

11

Some time before 1100 we hear of a professor named Pepo, " the bright and shining light of Bologna "; by 1119 we meet with the phrase *Bononia docta.* At Bologna, as at Paris, a great teacher stands at the beginning of university development. The teacher who gave Bologna its reputation was one Irnerius, perhaps the most famous of the many great professors of law in the Middle Ages. Just what he wrote and what he taught are still subjects of dispute among scholars, but he seems to have fixed the method of ' glossing ' the law texts upon the basis of a comprehensive use of the whole *Corpus Juris,* as contrasted with the meagre epitomes of the preceding centuries, fully and finally separating the Roman law from rhetoric and establishing it firmly as a subject of professional study. Then, about 1140, Gratian, a monk of San Felice, composed the *Decretum* which became the standard text in canon law, thus marked off from theology as a distinct subject of higher study; and the preëmi-

12

nence of Bologna as a law school was fully assured.

A student class had now appeared, expressing itself in correspondence and in poetry, and by 1158 it was sufficiently important in Italy to receive a formal grant of rights and privileges from Emperor Frederick Barbarossa, though no particular town or university is mentioned. By this time Bologna had become the resort of some hundreds of students, not only from Italy but from beyond the Alps. Far from home and undefended, they united for mutual protection and assistance, and this organization of foreign, or Transmontane, students was the beginning of the university. In this union they seem to have followed the example of the gilds already common in Italian cities. Indeed, the word university means originally such a group or corporation in general, and only in time did it come to be limited to gilds of masters and students, *universitas societas magistrorum discipulorumque.*

13

Historically, the word university has no connection with the universe or the universality of learning; it denotes only the totality of a group, whether of barbers, carpenters, or students did not matter. The students of Bologna organized such a university first as a means of protection against the townspeople, for the price of rooms and necessaries rose rapidly with the crowd of new tenants and consumers, and the individual student was helpless against such profiteering. United, the students could bring the town to terms by the threat of departure as a body, secession, for the university, having no buildings, was free to move, and there are many historic examples of such migrations. Better rent one's rooms for less than not rent them at all, and so the student organizations secured the power to fix the prices of lodgings and books through their representatives.

Victorious over the townsmen, the students turned on ' their other enemies, the

14

professors.' Here the threat was a collective boycott, and as the masters lived at first wholly from the fees of their pupils, this threat was equally effective. The professor was put under bond to live up to a minute set of regulations which guaranteed his students the worth of the money paid by each. We read in the earliest statutes (1317) that a professor might not be absent without leave, even a single day, and if he desired to leave town he had to make a deposit to ensure his return. If he failed to secure an audience of five for a regular lecture, he was fined as if absent — a poor lecture indeed which could not secure five hearers! He must begin with the bell and quit within one minute after the next bell. He was not allowed to skip a chapter in his commentary, or postpone a difficulty to the end of the hour, and he was obliged to cover ground systematically, so much in each specific term of the year. No one might spend the whole year on introduction and bibliography! Coercion of this sort presupposes an effective organization of the student body, and we hear of two and even four universities of students, each composed of ' nations ' and presided over by a rector. Emphatically Bologna was a student university, and Italian students are still quite apt to demand a voice in university affairs. When I first visited the University of Palermo I found it just recovering from a riot in which the students had broken the front windows in a demand for more frequent, and thus less comprehensive, examinations. At Padua's seventh centenary last May the students practically took over the town, with a programme of processions and ceremonies quite their own and an amount of noise and tumult which almost broke up the most solemn occasions and did break the windows of the greatest hall in the city.

Excluded from the ' universities ' of students, the professors also formed a gild or ' college,' requiring for admission thereto certain qualifications which were ascer-

16

tained by examination, so that no student could enter save by the gild's consent. And, inasmuch as ability to teach a subject is a good test of knowing it, the student came to seek the professor's license as a certificate of attainment, regardless of his future career. This certificate, the license to teach (*licentia docendi*), thus became the earliest form of academic degree. Our higher degrees still preserve this tradition in the words master (*magister*) and doctor, originally synonymous, while the French even have a *licence*. A Master of Arts was one qualified to teach the liberal arts; a Doctor of Laws, a certified teacher of law. And the ambitious student sought the degree and gave an inaugural lecture, even when he expressly disclaimed all intention of continuing in the teaching profession. Already we recognize at Bologna the standard academic degrees as well as the university organization and well-known officials like the rector.

Other subjects of study appeared in

course of time, arts, medicine, and theology, but Bologna was preëminently a school of civil law, and as such it became the model of university organization for Italy, Spain, and southern France, countries where the study of law has always had political and social as well as merely academic significance. Some of these universities became Bologna's competitors, like Montpellier and Orleans as well as the Italian schools nearer home. Frederick II founded the University of Naples in 1224 so that the students of his Sicilian kingdom could go to a Ghibelline school at home instead of the Guelfic centre in the North. Rival Padua was founded two years earlier as a secession from Bologna, and only last year, on the occasion of Padua's seven-hundredth anniversary, I saw the ancient feud healed by the kiss of peace bestowed on Bologna's rector amid the encores of ten thousand spectators. Padua, however, scarcely equalled Bologna in our period, even though at a later age Portia sent thither

18

for legal authority, and though the university still shines with the glory of Galileo.

In northern Europe the origin of universities must be sought at Paris, in the cathedral school of Notre-Dame. By the beginning of the twelfth century in France and the Low Countries learning was no longer confined to monasteries but had its most active centres in the schools attached to cathedrals, of which the most famous were those of Liège, Rheims, Laon, Paris, Orleans, and Chartres. The most notable of these schools of the liberal arts was probably Chartres, distinguished by a canonist like St. Ives and by famous teachers of classics and philosophy like Bernard and Thierry. As early as 991 a monk of Rheims, Richer, describes the hardships of his journey to Chartres in order to study the *Aphorisms* of Hippocrates of Cos; while from the twelfth century John of Salisbury, the leading northern humanist of the age, has left us an

19

account of the masters which we shall later have occasion to cite. Nowhere else today can we drop back more easily into a cathedral city of the twelfth century, the peaceful town still dominated by its church and sharing, now as then,

> the minster's vast repose.
> Silent and gray as forest-leaguered cliff
> Left inland by the ocean's slow retreat,
> . . . . patiently remote
> From the great tides of life it breasted once,
> Hearing the noise of men as in a dream.

By the time the cathedral stood complete, with its "dedicated shapes of saints and kings," it had ceased to be an intellectual centre of the first importance, overshadowed by Paris fifty-odd miles away, so that Chartres never became a university.

The advantages of Paris were partly geographical, partly political as the capital of the new French monarchy, but something must be set down to the influence of a great teacher in the person of Abelard. This brilliant young radical, with his persistent questioning and his scant respect for titled authority, drew students in large numbers wherever he taught, whether at Paris or in the wilderness. At Paris he was connected with the church of Mont-Sainte-Geneviève longer than with the cathedral school, but resort to Paris became a habit in his time, and in this way he had a significant influence on the rise of the university. In an institutional sense the university was a direct outgrowth of the school of Notre-Dame, whose chancellor alone had authority to license teaching in the diocese and thus kept his control over the granting of university degrees, which here as at Bologna were originally teachers' certificates. The early schools were within the cathedral precincts on the Ile de la Cité, that tangled quarter about Notre-Dame pictured by Victor Hugo which has long since been demolished. A little later we find masters and scholars living on the Little Bridge (Petit-Pont) which connected the island with the Left Bank of the Seine —

this bridge gave its name to a whole school of philosophers, the Parvipontani — but by the thirteenth century they have overrun the Left Bank, thenceforth the Latin Quarter of Paris.

At what date Paris ceased to be a cathedral school and became a university, no one can say, though it was certainly before the end of the twelfth century. Universities, however, like to have precise dates to celebrate, and the University of Paris has chosen 1200, the year of its first royal charter. In that year, after certain students had been killed in a town and gown altercation, King Philip Augustus issued a formal privilege which punished his prévôt and recognized the exemption of the students and their servants from lay jurisdiction, thus creating that special position of students before the courts which has not yet wholly disappeared from the world's practice, though generally from its law. More specific was the first papal privilege, the bull *Parens scientiarum* of 1231, issued after a two years' cessation of lectures growing out of a riot in which a band of students, having found " wine that was good and sweet to drink," beat up the tavern keeper and his friends till they in turn suffered from the prévôt and his men, a dissension in which the thirteenth century clearly saw the hand of the devil. Confirming the existing exemptions, the Pope goes on to regulate the discretion of the chancellor in conferring the license, at the same time that he recognizes the right of the masters and students " to make constitutions and ordinances regulating the manner and time of lectures and disputations, the costume to be worn," attendance at masters' funerals, the lectures of bachelors, necessarily more limited than those of fully fledged masters, the price of lodgings, and the coercion of members. Students must not carry arms, and only those who frequent the schools regularly are to enjoy the exemptions of students, the interpretation in practice being attendance at not less than two lectures a week.

While the word university does not appear in these documents, it is taken for granted. A university in the sense of an organized body of masters existed already in the twelfth century; by 1231 it had developed into a corporation, for Paris, in contrast to Bologna, was a university of masters. There were now four faculties, each under a dean: arts, canon law (civil law was forbidden at Paris after 1219), medicine, and theology. The masters of arts, much more numerous than the others, were grouped into four 'nations': the French, including the Latin peoples; the Norman; the Picard, including also the Low Countries; and the English, comprising England, Germany, and the North and East of Europe. These four nations chose the head of the university, the rector, as he is still generally styled on the Continent, whose term, however, was short, being later only three months. If we may judge from such minutes as have survived, much of the time of the nations was devoted to consuming the fees collected from new members and new officers, or, as it was called, drinking up the surplus — at the Two Swords near the Petit-Pont, at the sign of Our Lady in the Rue S.-Jacques, at the Swan, the Falcon, the Arms of France, and scores of similar places. A learned monograph on the taverns of mediaeval Paris has been written from the records of the English nation alone. The artificial constitution of the nations seems to have encouraged rather than diminished the feuds and rivalries between the various regions represented at Paris, of which Jacques de Vitry has left a classic description: [1]

" They wrangled and disputed not merely about the various sects or about some discussions; but the differences between the countries also caused dissensions, hatreds, and virulent animosities among them, and they impudently uttered all kinds of affronts and insults

[1] As translated by Munro, *The Mediaeval Student*, p. 19.

25

against one another. They affirmed that the English were drunkards and had tails; the sons of France proud, effeminate, and carefully adorned like women. They said that the Germans were furious and obscene at their feasts; the Normans, vain and boastful; the Poitevins, traitors and always adventurers. The Burgundians they considered vulgar and stupid. The Bretons were reputed to be fickle and changeable, and were often reproached for the death of Arthur. The Lombards were called avaricious, vicious, and cowardly; the Romans, seditious, turbulent, and slanderous; the Sicilians, tyrannical and cruel; the inhabitants of Brabant, men of blood, incendiaries, brigands, and ravishers; the Flemish, fickle, prodigal, gluttonous, yielding as butter, and slothful. After such insults, from words they often came to blows."

Another university institution which goes back to twelfth-century Paris is the college. Originally merely an endowed hospice or hall of residence, the college

early became an established unit of aca-
demic life at many universities. | " The
object of the earliest college-founders was
simply to secure board and lodging for
poor scholars who could not pay for it
themselves "; but in course of time the
colleges became normal centres of life and
teaching, absorbing into themselves much
of the activity of the university. The colleges had buildings and endowments, if
the university had not. | There was a col-
lege at Paris as early as 1180; there were
sixty-eight by 1500, and the system survived until the Revolution, to leave be-
hind it only fragments of buildings or
local names like the Sorbonne of today,
sole memento of that Collège de la Sorbonne founded for theologians by a con-
fessor of St. Louis in the thirteenth century. Many other continental universities had their colleges, one of which, the
ancient College of Spain at Bologna, still
survives for the delectation of the few
Spanish youths who reach its quiet court-
yard. But of course the ultimate home of

the college was Oxford and Cambridge, where it came to be the most characteristic feature of university life, arrogating to itself practically all teaching as well as direction of social life, until the university became merely an examining and degree-conferring body. Here the older colleges like Balliol, Merton, and Peterhouse date from the thirteenth century.

Paris was preëminent in the Middle Ages as a school of theology, and, as theology was the supreme subject of mediaeval study, " Madame la haute science " it was called, this means that it was preëminent as a university. " The Italians have the Papacy, the Germans have the Empire, and the French have Learning," ran the old saying; and the chosen abode of learning was Paris. Quite naturally Paris became the source and the model for northern universities. Oxford branched off from this parent stem late in the twelfth century, likewise with no definite date of foundation; Cambridge began somewhat later. The German universities, none of them older than the fourteenth century, were confessed imitations of Paris. Thus the Elector Palatine, Ruprecht, in founding the University of Heidelberg in 1386 — for these later universities were founded at specific dates — provides that it " shall be ruled, disposed, and regulated according to the modes and matters accustomed to be observed in the University of Paris, and that as a handmaid of Paris — a worthy one let us hope — it shall imitate the steps of Paris in every way possible, so that there shall be four faculties," four nations and a rector, exemptions for students and their servants, and even caps and gowns for the several faculties " as has been observed at Paris." [1]

By the end of the Middle Ages at least eighty universities had been founded in different parts of Europe.[2] Some of

[1] Translated in E. F. Henderson, *Select Historical Documents of the Middle Ages,* pp. 262–266.

[2] Table in Rashdall, *Universities,* I, p. xxviii; map at beginning of Vol. II and in Shepherd, *Historical Atlas* (New York, 1911), p. 100.

these were short-lived, many were of only
local importance, others like Salerno
flourished only to die, but some like Paris
and Montpellier, Bologna and Padua,
Oxford and Cambridge, Vienna and
Prague and Leipzig, Coimbra and Sa-
lamanca, Cracow and Louvain, have an
unbroken history of many centuries of
distinction. And the great European universities of more recent foundation, like
Berlin, Strasbourg, Edinburgh, Man-
chester, and London, follow in their organization the ancient models. In America the earliest institutions of higher learning reproduced the type of the contemporary English college at a time when the
university in England was eclipsed by
its constituent colleges; but in the crea-
tion of universities in the later nineteenth
century, America turned to the universities of the Continent and thus entered
once more into the ancient inheritance.
Even in the colonial period a sense of the
general university tradition survived, for
the charter of Rhode Island College in

1764 grants " the same privileges, dignities, and immunities enjoyed by the American colleges, and European universities."

What then is our inheritance from the oldest of universities? In the first place it is not buildings or a type of architecture, for the early universities had no buildings of their own, but on occasion used private halls and neighboring churches. After all, as late as 1775 the First Baptist Church in Providence was built " for the publick worship of Almighty God, and also for holding Commencement in " ! Indeed one who seeks to reconstruct the life of ancient universities will find little aid in their existing remains. Salerno retains no monuments of its university, though its rare old cathedral, where Hildebrand lies buried, must have seen the passing of many generations of would-be physicians. In the halls and coats of arms of " many-domed Padua proud " we behold the Renaissance, not the Middle Ages. Even Bologna, *Bononia docta,* with its leaning towers and cool arcades, has no remains of university architecture earlier than the fourteenth century, from which date the oldest monuments of its professors of law gathered now into the municipal museum. Montpellier and Orleans preserve nothing from this period. Paris, too often careless of its storied past, can show to-day only the ancient church of Saint-Julien-le-Pauvre, where university meetings were often held, unless we count, as we should, the great cathedral in the Cité whence the university originally sprang. The oldest Cambridge college, Peterhouse, has only a fragment of its earliest buildings; the finest Cambridge monument, King's College chapel, is of the late fifteenth century. More than all others Oxford gives the deepest impression of continuity with an ancient past, Matthew Arnold's Oxford, " so venerable, so lovely . . . steeped in sentiment as she lies, spreading her gardens to the moonlight, and whispering from her towers the last enchantments of the Middle Age " ; yet so far as the actual college buildings are concerned they have much more of sentiment than of the Middle Ages. Only at Merton, which fixed the college type at Oxford, do any of the present structures carry us back of 1300, and nowhere is there much of the fourteenth century. Those venerable glories of Oxford, the Bodleian library, the tower of Magdalen, and the hall of Christ Church, belong to a much later age, the period of the Tudors, and thus by ordinary reckoning to modern times. When we say how very mediaeval, we often mean how very Tudor!

Neither does the continuity lie in academic form and ceremony, in spite of occasional survivals, like the conferring of degrees by the ring or the kiss of peace, or the timing of examinations by the hour glass as I have seen it at Portuguese Coimbra. Academic costume has in it some element of tradition where it is a daily dress as at Oxford, Cambridge, and Coimbra, but in America the tradition was broken by our ancestors, and the formal cap and gown current in the United States today are a product of modern Albany rather than of mediaeval Paris and Bologna. Even in their ancient homes the costumes have changed. " It is probable," says Rashdall, " that no gown now worn in Oxford has much resemblance to its mediaeval ancestor." A student of mediaeval Padua would not recognize the variegated procession which wound through its streets last summer; Robert de Sorbon would rub his eyes at the non-mediaeval styles of the gorgeous gowns which were massed on the stage of the great hall of the Sorbonne when President Wilson received his honorary degree in 1918.

 It is, then, in institutions that the university tradition is most direct. First, the very name university, as an association of masters and scholars leading the common life of learning. Characteristic of the

Middle Ages as such a corporation is, the individualistic modern world has found nothing to take its place. Next, the notion of a curriculum of study, definitely laid down as regards time and subjects, tested by an examination and leading to a degree, as well as many of the degrees themselves — bachelor, as a stage toward the mastership, master, doctor, in arts, law, medicine, and theology. Then the faculties, four or more, with their deans, and the higher officers such as chancellors and rectors, not to mention the college, wherever the residential college still survives. The essentials of university organization are clear and unmistakable, and they have been handed down in unbroken continuity. They have lasted more than seven hundred years — what form of government has lasted so long? Very likely all this is not final — nothing is in this world of flux — but it is singularly tough and persistent, suited to use and also to abuse, like Bryce's university with a faculty " consisting of Mrs. Johnson and myself," or the " eleven leading universities " of a certain state of the Middle West! Universities are at times criticised for their aloofness or their devotion to vocationalism, for being too easy or too severe, and drastic efforts have been made to reform them by abolishing entrance requirements or eliminating all that does not lead directly to bread and butter; but no substitute has been found for the university in its main business, the training of scholars and the maintenance of the tradition of learning and investigation. The glory of the mediaeval university, says Rashdall, was " the consecration of Learning," and the glory and the vision have not yet perished from the earth. " The mediaeval university," it has been said, " was the school of the modern spirit." How the early universities performed this task will be the theme of the next lecture.

II

THE MEDIAEVAL PROFESSOR

In the last lecture we considered the mediaeval university as an institution. We come now to examine it as an intellectual centre. This involves some account of its course of study, its methods of teaching, and the status and freedom of its teachers. The element of continuity, so clear in institutions, is often less evident in the content of learning, but even here the thread is unbroken, the contrast with modern conditions less sharp than is often supposed.

The basis of education in the early Middle Ages consisted, as we have seen, of the so-called seven liberal arts. Three of these, grammar, rhetoric, and logic, were grouped as the trivium; the remaining four, arithmetic, geometry, astronomy, and music, made up the quadrivium. The first group was the more rudimentary, but the second was rudimentary enough. The number was fixed and the content standardized during the decadence of ancient learning, and the whole conception reached the Middle Ages chiefly in the book of a certain Martianus Capella, written in the early fifth century. These later ages of classical antiquity, in condensing and desiccating knowledge for their own more limited intelligence, were also unconsciously preparing for later times those small and convenient packages which alone could be carried as a *viaticum* through the stormy times of the Dark Ages. It was almost wholly as formulated in a few standard texts that the learning of the ancient world was transmitted to mediaeval times, and the authority of these manuals was so great that a list of those in use in any period affords an accurate index of the extent of its knowledge and the nature of its instruction. It was a bookish age, with great reverence for standard authorities, and its instruction followed closely the written word.

In the monastic and cathedral schools of the earlier period the text-books were few and simple, chiefly the Latin grammars of Donatus and Priscian with some elementary reading-books, the logical manuals of Boethius, as well as his arithmetic and music, a manual of rhetoric, the most elementary propositions of geometry, and an outline of practical astronomy such as that of the Venerable Bede. Of Greek, of course, there was none. This slender curriculum in arts was much enlarged by the renaissance of the twelfth century, which added to the store of western knowledge the astronomy of Ptolemy, the complete works of Euclid, and the Aristotelian logic, while at the same time under the head of grammar great stimulus was given to the study and reading of the Latin classics. This classical revival, which is noteworthy and comparatively little known, centred in such cathedral schools as Chartres and Orleans, where the spirit of a real humanism showed itself in an enthusiastic study of ancient authors and in the production of Latin verse of a really remarkable quality. Certain writings of one of these poets, Bishop Hildebert of Le Mans, were even mistaken for " real antiques " by later humanists. Nevertheless, though brilliant, this classical movement was short-lived, crushed in its early youth by the triumph of logic and the more practical studies of law and rhetoric. In the later twelfth century John of Salisbury inveighs against the logicians of his day, with their superficial knowledge of literature; in the university curriculum of the thirteenth century, literary studies have quite disappeared. Toward 1250, when a French poet, Henri d'Andeli, wrote his *Battle of the Seven Arts,* the classics are already the ancients, fighting a losing battle against the moderns:

> Logic has the students,
> Whereas Grammar is reduced in numbers.

.   .   .   .

THE MEDIAEVAL PROFESSOR

Civil Law rode gorgeously
And Canon Law rode haughtily
Ahead of all the other arts.

If the absence of the ancient classics and of vernacular literature is a striking feature of the university curriculum in arts, an equally striking fact is the amount of emphasis placed on logic or dialectic. The earliest university statutes, those of Paris in 1215, require the whole of Aristotle's logical works, and throughout the Middle Ages these remain the backbone of the arts course, so that Chaucer can speak of the study of logic as synonymous with attendance at a university —

That un-to logik hadde longe y-go.

In a sense this is perfectly just, for logic was not only a major subject of study itself, it pervaded every other subject as a method and gave tone and character to the mediaeval mind. Syllogism, disputation, the orderly marshalling of argu-

41

ments for and against specific theses, these became the intellectual habit of the age in law and medicine as well as in philosophy and theology. The logic, of course, was Aristotle's, and the other works of the philosopher soon followed, so that in the Paris course of 1254 we find also the *Ethics,* the *Metaphysics,* and the various treatises on natural science which had at first been forbidden to students. To Dante Aristotle had become " the Master of them that know," by virtue of the universality of his method no less than of his all-embracing learning. " The father of book knowledge and the grandfather of the commentator," no other writer appealed so strongly as Aristotle to the mediaeval reverence for the textbook and the mediaeval habit of formal thought. Doctrines like the eternity of matter which seemed dangerous to faith were explained away, and great and authoritative systems of theology were built up by the methods of the pagan philosopher. And all idea of literary form disappeared when everything depended on argument alone.

If the study of the classics became confined to examples and excerpts designed to illustrate the rules of grammar, rhetoric had a somewhat different fate by reason of its practical applications. The intellectual life of the Middle Ages was not characterized by spontaneous or widely diffused power of literary expression. Few were able to write, still fewer could compose a letter, and the professional scribes and notaries on whom devolved the greater part of the labor of mediaeval correspondence fastened upon the letter-writing of the period the stereotyped formalism of a conventional rhetoric. Regular instruction in the composition of letters and official acts was given in the schools and chanceries, and numerous professors, called *dictatores*, went about from place to place teaching this valuable art — " often and exceeding necessary for the clergy, for monks suitable, and for laymen honorable," as one rhetorician tells us. By the thirteenth century such masters had found a place in certain universities, especially in Italy and Southern France, and they advertised their wares in a way that has been compared to the claims of a modern business course — short and practical, with no time wasted on outgrown classical authors but everything fresh and snappy and up-to-date, ready to be applied the same day if need be! Thus one professor at Bologna derides the study of Cicero, whom he cannot recall having read, and promises to train his students in writing every sort of letter and official document which was demanded of the notaries and secretaries of his day. Since, as we shall see in the next lecture, such teachers specialized in the composition of student letters, chiefly skilful appeals to the parental purse, their practical utility was at once apparent. " Let us," says one writer, " take as our theme today that a poor and diligent student at Paris is to write his mother for necessary expenses." Would not every listener be sure that here at least he had found " the real thing " ? The professor of rhetoric might also be called in to draft a university prospectus, like the circular issued in 1229 by the masters of the new University of Toulouse setting forth its superiority to Paris — theologians teaching in the pulpits and preaching at the street corners, lawyers magnifying Justinian and physicians Galen, professors of grammar and logic, and musicians with their organs, lectures on the books of natural philosophy then forbidden at Paris, low prices, a friendly populace, the way now prepared by the extirpation of the thorns of heresy, a land flowing with milk and honey, Bacchus reigning in the vineyards and Ceres in the fields under the mild climate desired by the philosophers of old, with plenary indulgence for all masters and students. Who could resist such an appeal from the South?

With grammar and rhetoric reduced to a subordinate position and the studies of the quadrivium receiving but scant attention, the arts course was mainly a course in logic and philosophy, plus so much of the natural sciences as could be apprehended by the scholastic study of the " natural books " of Aristotle. Laboratories there were none until long after the Middle Ages were past, and of history and the social sciences nothing was heard in universities until still later. Hard, close drill on a few well-thumbed books was the rule. The course in arts led normally to the master's degree in six years, with the baccalaureate somewhere on the way. Graduation in arts was the common preparation for professional study, being regularly required for theology and usual for intending lawyers and physicians. A sound tradition, to which the American world has given too little attention!

Contrary to a common impression, there were relatively few students of theology in mediaeval universities, for a prescribed theological training for the priesthood came in only with the Counter-

Reformation. The requirements for admission were high; the course in theology itself was long; the books were costly. True, these books were commonly only the Bible and the *Sentences* of Peter Lombard, but the Bible in the Middle Ages might run into several volumes, especially when accompanied by gloss and commentary, and the copying of these by hand was a tedious and costly business. An ambitious student at Orleans who asks for money to buy a Bible and begin theology is advised by his father to turn rather to some lucrative profession. At the best, complain the Paris chancellors, students come late to theology, which should be the wife of their youth.

Medicine likewise was studied in books, chiefly Galen and Hippocrates with their Arabic translators and commentators, among whom Avicenna held the first place after the thirteenth century. Indeed Avicenna was still more firmly intrenched in the East, for as late as 1887 a majority of the native physicians in the

47

Persian capital " knew no medicine but that of Avicenna." [1] Except for some advance in anatomy and surgery at certain southern schools, like Bologna and Montpellier, the mediaeval universities made no contributions to medical knowledge, for no subject was less adapted to their prevailing method of verbal and syllogistic dogmatism.

In law the basis of all instruction was inevitably the *Corpus Juris Civilis* of Justinian, for the customary law of mediaeval Europe was never a subject of university study. The central book was the *Digest,* summarizing the ripest fruits of Roman legal science, and it was their mastery of the *Digest* that gives pre-eminence to the mediaeval civilians. They brought the resources of the whole *Corpus* to bear on each passage in an elaborate gloss, and they showed refinement and subtlety of legal thought analogous to that of the scholastic philosophers. After all, " law is a form of scholasticism." But

[1] E. G. Browne, *Arabian Medicine* (1921), p. 93.

whereas the scholastic method in philosophy has lost hold on much of the modern world, the work of the glossators still survives. " In many respects," says Rashdall,[1] " the work of the School of Bologna represents the most brilliant achievement of the intellect of mediaeval Europe. The mediaeval mind had, indeed, a certain natural affinity for the study and development of an already existing body of Law. The limitations of its knowledge of the past and of the material Universe were not, to any appreciable extent, a bar to the mastery of a Science which concerns itself simply with the business and the relations of every-day life. The Jurist received his Justinian on authority as the Theologian received the Canonical and Patristic writings, or the Philosopher his Aristotle, while he had the advantage of receiving it in the original language. It had only to be understood, to be interpreted, developed, and applied. . . . The works of these men are, perhaps, the only

[1] *Universities,* I, pp. 254–255.

productions of mediaeval learning to which the modern Professor of any science whatever may turn, not merely for the sake of their historical interest, not merely in the hope of finding ideas of a suggestive value, but with some possibility of finding a solution of the doubts, difficulties and problems which still beset the modern student."

The canon law was closely associated with the civil, indeed for many purposes it was desirable to graduate in both these subjects as a *Doctor utriusque juris,* or as we say a J.U.D. or an LL. D. Canon law was condemned by the theologians as a " lucrative " subject, which drew students away from pure learning toward the path of ecclesiastical preferment. By the thirteenth century the mediaeval church was a vast administrative machine which needed lawyers to run it, and a well-trained canonist had a good chance of rising to the highest dignities.[1]   No

[1] Sic heredes Gratiani
Student fieri decani,
Abbates, pontifices.

wonder canon law attracted the ambitious, the wealthy, even the idle, for at Paris we are told that the lazy students frequented the lectures of the canonists in the middle of the morning, rather than the other courses which began at six. The standard textbook in canon law was the *Decretum* of Gratian, supplemented by the decretals of subsequent popes, especially the great collection which Gregory IX in 1234 distributed to the principal universities. The methods of studying these texts were the same as in the civil law, giving rise to the rich canonistic literature of the later Middle Ages and the marginal glosses for which, according to Dante, " the Gospel and the great doctors are deserted."

Of the textbooks needed in all these subjects the university undertook to secure a supply at once sufficient, correct, and cheap, for the regulation of the book trade was one of the earliest and most valued of university privileges. As books were costly they were commonly rented, at a fixed price per quire, rather than owned; indeed the sale of books was hedged in by close restrictions designed to curb monopoly prices and to prevent their removal from town. The earliest Paris tariff, ca. 1286, lists for rent copies of one hundred and thirty-eight different books. In course of time many students came to have books of their own — a Bible, or at least some part of it, a piece of the *Digest,* perhaps even the " twenty bokes clad in blak or reed " of Chaucer's Oxford clerk. Whether rented or owned, the supply was not inconsiderable; on the Bolognese monuments each student has a book before him. So long as each copy had to be made by hand, accuracy was a matter of much importance, and the university had its supervisors and correctors who inspected periodically all the books for sale in the town. Moreover, at Bologna a constant supply of new books was secured by the requirement that every professor should turn over a copy of his repetitions and disputations to the stationers for publication. The principal books of law and theology were the natural outgrowth of university lectures. With demand and supply so largely concentrated in the universities, it is not surprising that these should have become the chief centres of the book trade and, as we should say, of the publishing business. So long as students could rent the books they required, there was less need for libraries than we might at first suppose, and it was quite natural that for long the university as such should have no library. In course of time, however, books were given for the use of students, chiefly in the form of bequests to the colleges, where they could be borrowed or consulted on the spot. By 1338 the oldest extant catalogue of the Sorbonne, the chief Paris library, lists 1722 volumes, many of them still to be seen in the Bibliothèque Nationale, while many an Oxford college still preserves codices which belonged to its library in the Middle Ages.

Turning from books to professors, we should note at the outset that the Middle Ages produced many excellent and renowned teachers. The mechanism of learning was still comparatively simple, its content not yet overwhelming, and, in spite of the close adherence to texts, there was a large scope for the personality of the instructor. Thus, long before the days of universities, Alcuin was the moving spirit in the revival of education at the court of Charlemagne and the monastery school of Tours, and two centuries later Gerbert of Rheims roused the wonder of contemporaries by his skilful use of the classics in the study of rhetoric and by devices for the teaching of astronomy so ingenious that they seemed in some way "divine." [1] From the period of university origins we get a fairly clear impression of Abelard as a teacher and 'classroom entertainer,' bold, original, lucid,

[1] Richer, I, cc. 45–54; extracts translated in Taylor, *Mediaeval Mind* (1919), I, pp. 289–293.

sharply polemical, always fresh and stimulating, and withal "able to move to laughter the minds of serious men." His procedure as exhibited in his *Sic et non* was to marshal authorities and arguments for and against specific propositions, a method which was soon imitated in Gratian's *Concord of Discordant Canons,* and, reënforced by the *New Logic* of Aristotle, was to culminate in the scholastic method of St. Thomas Aquinas and stamp itself upon the thought of many generations. Sharpening to the wits as this method was in the hands of Abelard and his successors, the very antagonism of yes or no as he formulated it left no room for intermediate positions, for those *nuances* of thought in which, as Renan pointed out, truth is usually to be found.

For a contemporary impression of the teachers of the twelfth century, nothing is so good as the oft-quoted passages in which John of Salisbury describes his *Wanderjahre* in France from 1136 to

1147, chiefly at Paris and Chartres.[1]
Learning the rudiments of dialectic from
Abelard, he continued under two other
teachers of this art, one over-scrupulous
in detail, perspicuous, brief, and to the
point, the other subtle and profuse, show-
ing that simple answers could not be
given. " Afterward one of them went to
Bologna and unlearned what he had
taught, so that on his return he also un-
taught it." John then passed on to
Chartres to study grammar under William
of Conches and Bernard. The humane
yet thorough teaching of literature here
excited his warm admiration — close
study, memorizing choice extracts, grammar taught by composition, imitation of
excellent models but merciless exposure of
borrowed finery, qualities which made Bernard " the most copious source of letters

[1] Translated in R. L. Poole, *Illustrations of the
History of Mediaeval Thought,* pp. 203–212;
A. O. Norton, *Readings in the History of Education,* pp. 28–34. What we know of these masters
is analyzed by Poole in the *English Historical Re-
view,* xxxv, pp. 321–342 (1920).

in Gaul in modern times." Returning to Paris after twelve years' absence, John found his old companions " as before, and where they were before; nor did they appear to have reached the goal in unravelling the old questions, nor had they added one jot of a proposition. The aims that once inspired them, inspired them still: they had progressed in one point only: they had unlearned moderation, they knew not modesty; in such wise that one might despair of their recovery. And thus experience taught me a manifest conclusion, that, whereas dialectic furthers other studies, so if it remain by itself it lies bloodless and barren, nor does it quicken the soul to yield fruit of philosophy, except the same conceive from elsewhere."

The teachers of the thirteenth century who talk most about themselves are the professors of grammar and rhetoric like Buoncompagno at Bologna, John of Garlande at Paris, Ponce of Provence at Orleans, and Lorenzo of Aquileia at Naples and almost everywhere, but we shall make sufficient acquaintance with their inflated writings in other connections. More significant is the account which Odofredus gives of his lectures on the *Old Digest* at Bologna:

" Concerning the method of teaching the following order was kept by ancient and modern doctors and especially by my own master, which method I shall observe: First, I shall give you summaries of each title before I proceed to the text; second, I shall give you as clear and explicit a statement as I can of the purport of each law [included in the title]; third, I shall read the text with a view to correcting it; fourth, I shall briefly repeat the contents of the law; fifth, I shall solve apparent contradictions, adding any general principles of law [to be extracted from the passage], commonly called ' Brocardica,' and any distinctions or subtle and useful problems (*quaestiones*) arising out of the law with their solutions, as far as the Divine Providence shall enable me. And if any law shall seem de-

58

serving, by reason of its celebrity or difficulty, of a repetition, I shall reserve it for an evening repetition, for I shall dispute at least twice a year, once before Christmas and once before Easter, if you like.

" I shall always begin the *Old Digest* on or about the octave of Michaelmas [6 October] and finish it entirely, by God's help, with everything ordinary and extraordinary, about the middle of August. The *Code* I shall always begin about a fortnight after Michaelmas and by God's help complete it, with everything ordinary and extraordinary, about the first of August. Formerly the doctors did not lecture on the extraordinary portions; but with me all students can have profit, even the ignorant and the new-comers, for they will hear the whole book, nor will anything be omitted as was once the common practice here. For the ignorant can profit by the statement of the case and the exposition of the text, the more advanced can become more adept in the subtleties of questions and opposing opinions. And I shall read all the glosses, which was not the practice before my time." Then comes certain general advice as to the choice of teachers and the methods of study, followed by some general account of the *Digest*.

This course closed as follows: " Now gentlemen, we have begun and finished and gone through this book as you know who have been in the class, for which we thank God and His Virgin Mother and all His saints. It is an ancient custom in this city that when a book is finished mass should be sung to the Holy Ghost, and it is a good custom and hence should be observed. But since it is the practice that doctors on finishing a book should say something of their plans, I will tell you something but not much. Next year I expect to give ordinary lectures well and lawfully as I always have, but no extraordinary lectures, for students are not good payers, wishing to learn but not to pay, as the saying is: All desire to know but none to pay the price. I have nothing more to say to you beyond dismissing you with God's blessing and begging you to attend the mass." [1]

Important as was the formal lecture in those days of few books and no laboratories, it was by no means the sole vehicle of instruction. A comprehensive survey of university teaching would need also to take account of the less formal ' cursory ' or ' extraordinary ' lectures, many of them given by mere bachelors; the reviews and ' repetitions,' which were often given in hospices or colleges in the evenings; and the disputations which prepared for the final ordeal of maintaining publicly the graduation thesis.

The class-rooms in which these lectures were given have long since disappeared. If the master's house had no suitable room, he literally hired a hall in some con-

---

[1] Paris, Bibliothèque Nationale, MS. Lat. 4489, f. 102; Savigny, *Geschichte des römischen Rechts im Mittelalter* (1834), III, pp. 264, 541, 553; cf. Rashdall, I, p. 219.

venient neighborhood. At Paris such halls were mostly in a single street on the Left Bank, the Vicus Stramineus or Rue du Fouarre celebrated by Dante, apparently so-called from the straw-covered floor on which the students sat as they took notes. At Bologna the class-rooms were rather more ambitious. Here Buoncompagno, writing in 1235, has described an ideal lecture hall, quiet and clean, with a fair prospect from its windows, its walls painted green but with no pictures or statues to distract attention, the lecturer's seat elevated so that he may see and be seen by all, the seats of the students permanently assigned by nations and according to individual rank and fame; but he adds significantly, " I never had such a house myself and do not believe any of this sort was ever built." Our knowledge of the realities of the Bolognese class-room is derived chiefly from the monuments and miniatures of the professors of the fourteenth and fifteenth centuries, in which the master is regularly seated at a desk under a canopy on a raised platform, while the students have flat or inclined desks on which their books lie open. The professors, in medicine as in law, regularly have an open volume before them.

The nature of the final examination is best illustrated at Paris, where it is described in the *De conscientia* of that genial moralist, Robert de Sorbon, founder of the Sorbonne, by means of a suggestive parallel with the Last Judgment. Taking as his text Job's desire that his " adversary had written a book," and outlining his headings in the approved fashion of his time, Robert begins with the statement that if any one decides to seek the *licentia legendi* at Paris and cannot be excused from examination — as many of the great, by special favor, are — he would much like to be told by the chancellor, or by some one in his confidence, on what book he would be examined. Just as he would be a crazy student indeed, who, having found out which book this was, should neglect it and spend his time on others, even so is he mad who fails to study the book of his own conscience, in which we shall all, without exception, be examined at the great day. Moreover, if any one is rejected by the chancellor, he may be re-examined after a year, or it may be that, through the intercession of friends or by suitable gifts or services to the chancellor's relatives or other examiners, the chancellor can be induced to change his decision; whereas at the Last Judgment the sentence will be final and there will be no help from wealth or influence or stout assertion of ability as canonist or civilian or of familiarity with all arguments and all fallacies. Then, if one fails before the chancellor of Paris, the fact is known to but five or six and the mortification passes away in time, while the Great Chancellor, God, will refute the sinner ' in full university ' before the whole world. The chancellor, too, does not flog the candidate, but in the Last Judgment the guilty will be beaten with a rod of iron from the valley of Jehosaphat through the length of hell, nor can we reckon, like idle boys in the grammar-schools, on escaping Saturday's punishment by feigning illness, playing truant, or being stronger than the master, or like them solace ourselves with the thought that after all our fun is well worth a whipping. The chancellor's examination, too, is voluntary; he does not force any one to seek the degree, but waits as long as the scholars wish, and is even burdened with their insistent demands for examinations. In studying the book of our conscience we should imitate the candidates for the license, who eat and drink sparingly, conning steadily the one book they are preparing, searching out all the authorities that pertain to this, and hearing only the professors that lecture on this subject, so that they have difficulty in concealing from their fellows the fact that they are preparing for examination. Such preparation is not the work of five or ten days — though there are many who will not meditate a day or an hour on their sins — but of many years. At the examination the chancellor asks, " Brother, what do you say to this question, what do you say to this one and this one? " The chancellor is not satisfied with a verbal knowledge of books without an understanding of their sense, but unlike the Great Judge, who will hear the book of our conscience from beginning to end and suffer no mistakes, he requires only seven or eight passages in a book and passes the candidate if he answers three questions out of four. Still another difference lies in the fact that the chancellor does not always conduct the examination in person, so that the student who would be terrified in the presence of so much learning often answers well before the masters who act in the chancellor's place. Nothing is here said of the public maintenance of a thesis against all comers, an important final exercise which still survives as a form in German universities.

At Bologna there was first a " rigorous and tremendous examination " before doctors, each sworn to treat the candidate

" as he would his own son." Then followed a public examination and inception which a letter home described as follows: " ' Sing unto the Lord a new song, praise him with stringed instruments and organs, rejoice upon the high-sounding cymbals,' for your son has held a glorious disputation, which was attended by a great multitude of teachers and scholars. He answered all questions without a mistake, and no one could prevail against his arguments. Moreover he celebrated a famous banquet, at which both rich and poor were honored as never before, and he has duly begun to give lectures which are already so popular that others' class-rooms are deserted and his own are filled." The same rhetorician also tells of an unsuccessful candidate who could do nothing in the disputation but sat in his chair like a goat while the spectators in derision called him rabbi; his guests at the banquet had such eating that they had no will to drink, and he must needs hire students to attend his classes.

The social position of mediaeval professors must be seen against the background of the social system of a different age from ours. We come perhaps nearest to modern conditions in the cities of Italy, where there is evidence in the Middle Ages as now of the distinguished position of many professors of medicine and civil law. Many theologians and teachers of canon law reached high places in the church such as bishoprics and cardinalates. Among the theologians and philosophers those of highest distinction were regularly university professors: Thomas Aquinas, Albertus Magnus, Bonaventura, all the great array of doctors angelic, invincible, irrefragable, seraphic, subtle, and universal. That these were also Dominicans or Franciscans withdrew them only partially from the world.

If, as some reformers maintain, the social position and self-respect of professors involve their management of university affairs, the Middle Ages were the great age of professorial control. The

university itself was a society of masters
when it was not a society of students. As
there were no endowments of importance
there were no boards of trustees, nor was
there any such system of state control as
exists on the Continent or in many parts
of the United States. Administration in
the modern sense was strikingly absent,
but much time was consumed in various
sorts of university meetings. In a quite
remarkable degree the university was
self-governing as well as self-respecting,
escaping some of the abuses of a system
which occasionally allows trustees or regents to speak of professors as their
" hired men." Whether the individual
professor was freer under such a system
is another question, for the corporation of
masters was apt to exercise a pretty close
control over action if not over opinion,
and the tyranny of colleagues is a form of
that " tyranny of one's next-door neighbor " from which the world seems unable
to escape.

There remains the question of the professor's intellectual liberty, the right to teach truth as he sees it, which we have come to call academic freedom. It is plain that much depends here, as with Pilate, on our conception of truth. If it is something to be discovered by search, the search must be free and untrammelled. If, however, truth is something which has already been revealed to us by authority, then it has only to be expounded, and the expositor must be faithful to the authoritative doctrine. Needless to say, the latter was the mediaeval conception of truth and its teaching. " Faith," it was held, " precedes science, fixes its boundaries, and prescribes its conditions." [1] " I believe in order that I may know, I do not know in order to believe," said Anselm. If reason has its bounds thus set, it befits reason to be humble. Let not the masters and students of Paris, says Gregory IX, " show themselves philosophers, but let them strive to become God's learned." The dangers of intellectual pride and reliance

[1] Alzog, *Church History* (1876), II, p. 733.

upon reason alone are illustrated by many characteristic stories of masters struck dumb in the midst of their boasting, like Étienne de Tournay, who, having proved the doctrine of the Trinity " so lucidly, so elegantly, so catholically," asserted that he could just as easily demolish his own proof. Mediaeval orthodoxy looked askance at mere cleverness, partly because much of the discussion of the schools led nowhere, partly because a mind that played too freely about a proposition might easily fall into heresy. And for the detection and punishment of heresy the mediaeval church organized a special system of courts known as the Inquisition.

Such being the general conditions, what was the actual situation? In practice freedom was general, save in philosophy and theology. In law, in medicine, in grammar and mathematics, men were normally free to lecture and dispute as they would. As there was no social problem in the modern sense and no teaching of the social sciences as such, a fruitful source of difficulty was absent. So far as I know, no mediaeval professor was condemned for preaching free trade or free silver or socialism or non-resistance. Moreover, while individual treatises might be publicly burnt, as in the later Roman Empire, there was no organized censorship of books before the sixteenth century.

Now as to philosophy and theology. The trouble lies of course with theology, for philosophy was free save when it touched theological questions. But then, philosophy is very apt to touch theological questions, and all through the twelfth and thirteenth centuries there was an intermittent fight between Christian theology and pagan philosophy as represented by the works of Aristotle. It began with Abelard when he tried to apply his logical method of inquiry to theology, and it went on when his contemporary, Gilbert de la Porrée, directed still more of the Aristotelian logic toward theological speculation. By the end of the twelfth century, the *New Logic* was pretty well assimilated, but then came Aristotle's *Metaphysics* and natural philosophy, with their Arabic commentators, the study of which at Paris was formally forbidden in 1210 and 1215. In 1231 the Pope requires them to be "examined and purged of all suspicion of error," but by 1254 they are a fixed part of the curriculum in arts, not expurgated but reconciled by interpretation to the Christian faith. A generation later there is a recrudescence of Averroism, emphasizing the doctrine of the eternity of matter and the determination of earthly acts by the heavenly bodies; and two hundred and nineteen errors of this party were condemned in 1277 by the bishop of Paris, who took occasion to lament incursions into theology on the part of students of arts. Throughout this period the whole of Aristotle was taught and studied at Paris, and his method was used by Thomas Aquinas to rear his vast structure of scholastic theology. Others reserved for themselves a wide range of philosophic speculation, and in case of trouble they could save themselves by falling back on the doctrine that what was true in philosophy might be false in theology, and *vice versa*.

With an eye to this question of freedom of teaching, I have gone through all the documents of the thirteenth century in the Paris *Chartularium*. Outside of the great controversies just mentioned the result is meagre. In 1241 a series of ten errors was examined and condemned by the chancellor and the professors of theology, a very abstract series of propositions dealing with the visibility of the divine essence, angels, and the exact abiding-place of glorified souls in the next world, whether in the empyrean or the crystalline heaven. In 1247 it appears that a certain Master Raymond had been imprisoned for his errors by the advice of the masters of theology, and one John de Brescain had been deprived of his right to teach because of certain errors in logic " which seemed to come near Arian heresy," thus confusing the subjects of the two faculties, whose bounds had been set by the fathers. In and about 1255 Paris was in a ferment over the so-called 'Eternal Gospel,' an apocalyptic treatise which foretold a new era of the Spirit, beginning in 1260, in which the New Testament, the Pope, and the hierarchy should be superseded. Accepted by certain advanced Franciscans, these doctrines became the occasion of a long conflict with the Mendicant orders, but with no very decisive results. In 1277 Paris received notice of thirty errors in arts condemned at Oxford, not as heretical but as sufficient to cause the deposition of the master teaching them; but when we find among them the abolition of the cases of Latin nouns and the personal endings of verbs (*ego currit, tu currit,* etc.), we are likely to sympathize more with their unfortunate students than with the deposed masters. One is reminded of the modern definition of academic freedom as " the right to say what one thinks without thinking what one says!"

With these as the only notable examples of interference with free teaching at the storm centre of theological speculation in the most active period of its history, we must infer that there was a large amount of actual freedom. Trouble arose almost entirely out of what was deemed theological heresy, or undue meddling with theological subjects by those who lacked theological training. Those who stuck to their job seem generally to have been let alone. As the great jurist Cujas replied in the sixteenth century when asked whether he was Protestant or Catholic, *Nihil hoc ad edictum praetoris.* Even within the more carefully guarded field of theology and philosophy, it is doubtful whether many found themselves cramped. Accepting the principle of authority as their starting-point, men did not feel its limitations as we should feel them now. A fence is no obstacle to those who do not desire to go outside, and many barriers that would seem intolerable to a more sceptical age were not felt as barriers by the schoolmen. He is free who feels himself free.

Furthermore, for those accustomed to the wide diversities of the modern world, it is easy to form a false impression of the uniformity and sameness of mediaeval thought. Scholasticism was not one thing but many, as its historians constantly remind us, and the contests between different schools and shades of opinion were as keen as among the Greeks or in our own day. And if the differences often seem minute or unreal to our distant eye, we can make them modern enough by turning, for example, to the old question of the nature of universal conceptions, which divided the Nominalists and Realists of the Middle Ages. Are universals mere names, or have they a real existence, independent of their individual embodiments? A bit arid it all sounds if we make it merely a matter of logic, but exciting enough as soon as it becomes a question of life. The essence of the **Ref**-ormation lies implicit in whether we take a nominalist or a realist view of the church; the central problem of politics depends largely upon a nominalist or a realist view of the state. Upon the two sides of this last question millions of men have " all uncouthly died," all unconsciously too, no doubt, in the majority of cases, unaware of the ultimate issues of political authority for which they fought, but yet able to comprehend them when expressed in the concrete form of putting the interest of the state above the interest of its members.

In his own time and his own way the mediaeval professor often dealt with permanent human interests as he sharpened men's wits and kept alive the continuous tradition of learning.

III

THE MEDIAEVAL STUDENT

" A University," it has more than once been remarked by professors, " would be a very comfortable place were it not for the students." So far we have been considering universities from the point of view of professors; it is now the turn of the students, for whether these be regarded as a necessary evil or as the main reason for the university's existence, they certainly cannot be ignored. A mediaeval university was no regiment of colonels but " a society of masters *and scholars*," and to this second and more numerous element we must now direct our attention.

The mediaeval student is a more elusive figure than his teachers, for he is individually less conspicuous and must generally be seen in the mass. Moreover the mass is much diversified in time and space, so that generalization is difficult, what is true of one age and one university being quite untrue of other times and places. Even within the briefer span of American universities there are wide differences among the students of, let us say, Harvard in the seventeenth century, William and Mary in the eighteenth century, California in the nineteenth century, and Columbia in the twentieth century; and it would be impossible to make a true picture out of elements drawn indiscriminately from such disparate sources. Until the conditions at each university of the Middle Ages shall have been studied chronologically, no sound account of student life in general can be written, and this preliminary labor has nowhere been systematically attempted. At present we can do no more than indicate the principal sources of our information and the kind of light they throw upon student life.

Fortunately, out of the scattered remains of mediaeval times, there has come down to us a considerable body of material which deals, more or less directly, with student affairs. There are, for one thing, the records of the courts of law, which, amid the monotonous detail of petty disorders and oft-repeated offences, preserve now and then a vivid bit of mediaeval life — like the case of the Bolognese student who was attacked with a cutlass in a class-room, to the great damage and loss of those assembled to hear the lecture of a noble and egregious doctor of laws; or the student in 1289 who was set upon in the street in front of a lecture-room by a certain scribe, "who wounded him on the head with a stone, so that much blood gushed forth," while two companions gave aid and counsel, saying, "Give it to him, hit him," and when the offence had been committed ran away. So the coroners' rolls of Oxford record many a fatal issue of town and gown riots, while a recently published register of 1265 and 1266 shows the students of Bologna actively engaged in raising money by loans and by the sale of text-books. There are of course the university and college statutes, with their prohibitions and fines, regulating the subjects of conversation, the shape and color of caps and gowns, that academic dress which looks to us so mediaeval and is, especially in its American form, so very modern; careful also of the weightier matters of the law, like the enactment of New College against throwing stones in chapel, or the graded penalties at Leipzig for him who picks up a missile to throw at a professor, him who throws and misses, and him who accomplishes his fell purpose to the master's hurt. The chroniclers, too, sometimes interrupt their narrative of the affairs of kings and princes to tell of students and their doings, although their attention, like that of their modern successors, the newspapers, is apt to be caught by outbreaks of student lawlessness rather than by the wholesome routine of academic life.

Then we have the preachers of the time,

82

many of them also professors, whose sermons contain frequent allusions to student customs; indeed if further evidence were needed to dispel the illusion that the mediaeval university was devoted to biblical study and religious nurture, the Paris preachers of the period would offer sufficient proof. " The student's heart is in the mire," says one of them, " fixed on prebends and things temporal and how to satisfy his desires." " They are so litigious and quarrelsome that there is no peace with them; wherever they go, be it Paris or Orleans, they disturb the country, their associates, even the whole university." Many of them go about the streets armed, attacking the citizens, breaking into houses, and abusing women. They quarrel among themselves over dogs, women, or what-not, slashing off one another's fingers with their swords, or, with only knives in their hands and nothing to protect their tonsured pates, rush into conflicts from which armed knights would hold back. Their com-

patriots come to their aid, and soon whole
nations of students may be involved in
the fray. These Paris preachers take us
into the very atmosphere of the Latin
quarter and show us much of its varied
activity. We hear the cries and songs
of the streets —

> Li tens s' en veit,
> Et je n' ei riens fait;
> Li tens revient,
> Et je ne fais riens —

the students' tambourines and guitars,
their " light and scurrilous words," their
hisses and handclappings and loud shouts
of applause at sermons and disputations.
We watch them as they mock a neighbor
for her false hair or stick out their tongues
and make faces at the passers-by. We
see the student studying by his window,
talking over his future with his room-
mate, receiving visits from his parents,
nursed by friends when he is ill, singing
psalms at a student's funeral, or visiting
a fellow-student and asking him to visit

84

him — " I have been to see you, now come to our hospice."

All types are represented. There is the poor student, with no friend but St. Nicholas, seeking such charity as he can find or earning a pittance by carrying holy water or copying for others, in a fair but none too accurate hand, sometimes too poor to buy books or afford the expense of a course in theology, yet usually surpassing his more prosperous fellows who have an abundance of books at which they never look. There is the well-to-do student, who besides his books and desk will be sure to have a candle in his room and a comfortable bed with a soft mattress and luxurious coverings, and will be tempted to indulge the mediaeval fondness for fine raiment beyond the gown and hood and simple wardrobe prescribed by the statutes. Then there are the idle and aimless, drifting about from master to master and from school to school, and never hearing full courses or regular lectures. Some, who care only for the name of scholar and the income which they receive while attending the university, go to class but once or twice a week, choosing by preference the lectures on canon law, which leave them plenty of time for sleep in the morning. Many eat cakes when they ought to be at study, or go to sleep in the class-rooms, spending the rest of their time drinking in taverns or building castles in Spain (*castella in Hispania*); and when it is time to leave Paris, in order to make some show of learning such students get together huge volumes of calfskin, with wide margins and fine red bindings, and so with wise sack and empty mind they go back to their parents. " What knowledge is this," asks the preacher, " which thieves may steal, mice or moths eat up, fire or water destroy? " and he cites an instance where the student's horse fell into a river, carrying all his books with him. Some never go home, but continue to enjoy in idleness the fruits of their benefices. Even in vacation time, when

the rich ride off with their servants and
the poor trudge home under the burning
sun, many idlers remain in Paris to their
own and the city's harm. Mediaeval
Paris, we should remember, was not only
the incomparable " parent of the sciences,"
but also a place of good cheer and good
fellowship and varied delights, a favorite
resort not only of the studious but of
country priests on a holiday; and it would
not be strange if sometimes scholars pro-
longed their stay unduly and lamented
their departure in phrases which are something more than rhetorical commonplace.

Then the student is not unknown to the
poets of the period, among whom Ru-
tebeuf gives a picture of thirteenth-
century Paris not unlike that of the
sermonizers, while in the preceding century Jean de Hauteville shows the misery
of the poor and diligent scholar falling
asleep over his books, and Nigel " Wire-
ker " satirizes the English students at
Paris in the person of an ass, Brunellus,
— " Daun Burnell " in Chaucer — who

studies there seven years without learning a word, braying at the end as at the beginning of his course, and leaving at last with the resolve to become a monk or a bishop. Best of all is Chaucer's incomparable portrait of the clerk of Oxenford, hollow, threadbare, unworldly —

> For him was lever have at his beddes heed
> Twenty bokes, clad in blak or reed,
> Of Aristotle and his philosophye,
> Than robes riche, or fithele, or gay sautrye.
>
> . . . .
>
> Souninge in moral vertu was his speche,
> And gladly wolde he lerne, and gladly teche.

But after all, no one knows so much about student life as the students themselves, and it is particularly from what was written by and for them, the student literature of the Middle Ages, that I wish to draw more at length. Such remains of the academic past fall into three chief classes: student manuals, student letters, and student poetry. Let us consider them in this order.

The manuals of general advice and counsel addressed to the mediaeval scholar do not call for extended consideration. Formal treatises on the whole duty of students are characteristic of the didactic habit of mind of the Middle Ages, but the advice which they contain is apt to be of a very general sort, applicable to one age as well as another and lacking in those concrete illustrations which enliven the sermons of the period into useful sources for university life.

A more interesting type of student manual, the student dictionary, owes its existence to the position of Latin as the universal language of mediaeval education. Text-books were in Latin, lectures were in Latin, and, what is more, the use of Latin was compulsory in all forms of student intercourse. This rule may have been designed as a check on conversation, as well as an incentive to learning, but it was enforced by penalties and informers (called wolves), and the freshman, or yellow-beak, as he was termed in mediae-val parlance, might find himself but ill equipped for making himself understood in his new community. For his con-venience a master in the University of Paris in the thirteenth century, John of Garlande, prepared a descriptive vocabu-lary, topically arranged and devoting a large amount of space to the objects to be seen in the course of a walk through the streets of Paris. The reader is con-ducted from quarter to quarter and from trade to trade, from the book-stalls of the Parvis Notre-Dame and the fowl-market of the adjoining Rue Neuve to the money-changers' tables and goldsmiths' shops on the Grand-Pont and the bow-makers of the Porte S.-Lazare, not omit-ting the classes of *ouvrières* whose ac-quaintance the student was most likely to make. Saddlers and glovers, furriers, cobblers, and apothecaries, the clerk might have use for the wares of all of them, as well as the desk and candle and writing-materials which were the special tools of his calling; but his most frequent relations were with the purveyors of food and drink, whose agents plied their trade vigorously through the streets and lanes of the Latin quarter and worked off their poorer goods on scholars and their servants. There were the hawkers of wine, crying their samples of different qualities from the taverns; the fruit-sellers, deceiving clerks with lettuce and cress, cherries, pears, and green apples; and at night the vendors of light pastry, with their carefully covered baskets of wafers, waffles, and rissoles — a frequent stake at the games of dice among students, who had a custom of hanging from their windows the baskets gained by lucky throws of the six. The *pâtissiers* had also more substantial wares suited to the clerical taste, tarts filled with eggs and cheese and well-peppered pies of pork, chicken, and eels. To the *rôtissiers* scholars' servants resorted, not only for the pigeons, geese, and other fowl roasted on their spits, but also for uncooked beef, pork, and mutton, seasoned with garlic and other strong sauces. Such fare, however, was not for the poorer students, whose slender purses limited them to tripe and various kinds of sausage, over which a quarrel might easily arise and "the butchers be themselves butchered by angry scholars."

A dictionary of this sort easily passes into another type of treatise, the manual of conversation. This method of studying foreign languages is old, as survivals from ancient Egypt testify, and it still spreads its snares for the unwary traveller who prepares to conquer Europe *à la* Ollendorff. To the writers of the later Middle Ages it seemed to offer an exceptional opportunity for combining Instruction in Latin with sound academic discipline, and from both school and university it left its monuments for our perusal. The most interesting of these handbooks is entitled a "Manual of Scholars who propose to attend universities of students and to profit therein," and while in its most common form it is designed for the students of Heidelberg about the year 1480, it could be adapted with slight changes to any of the German universities. " Rollo at Heidelberg," we might call it. Its eighteen chapters conduct the student from his matriculation to his degree, and inform him by the way on many subjects quite unnecessary for either. When the young man arrives he registers from Ulm; his parents are in moderate circumstances; he has come to study. He is then duly hazed after the German fashion, which treats the candidate as an unclean beast with horns and tusks which must be removed by officious fellow-students, who also hear his confession of sin and fix as the penance a good dinner for the crowd. He begins his studies by attending three lectures a day, and learns to champion nominalism against realism and the comedies of Terence against the law, and to discuss the advantages of various universities and the price of food and the quality of

the beer in university towns. Then we
find him and his room-mate quarrelling
over a mislaid book; rushing at the first
sound of the bell to dinner, where they
debate the relative merits of veal and
beans; or walking in the fields beyond the
Neckar, perhaps by the famous Philosophers' Road which has charmed so many
generations of Heidelberg youth, and
exchanging Latin remarks on the birds
and fish as they go. Then there are
shorter dialogues: the scholar breaks the
statutes; he borrows money, and gets it
back; he falls in love and recovers; he
goes to hear a fat Italian monk preach or
to see the jugglers and the jousting in
the market-place; he knows the dog-days
are coming — he can feel them in his
head! Finally our student is told by his
parents that it is high time for him to
take his degree and come home. At this
he is much disturbed; he has gone to few
lectures, and he will have to swear that
he has attended regularly; he has not
worked much and has incurred the enmity

of many professors; his master discourages him from trying the examination; he fears the disgrace of failure. But his interlocutor reassures him by a pertinent quotation from Ovid and suggests that a judicious distribution of gifts may do much — a few florins will win him the favor of all. Let him write home for more money and give a great feast for his professors; if he treats them well, he need not fear the outcome. This advice throws a curious light upon the educational standards of the time; it appears to have been followed, for the manual closes with a set of forms inviting the masters to the banquet and the free bath by which it was preceded.

If university students had need of such elementary compends of morals and manners, there was obviously plenty of room for them in the lower schools as well, where they were apt to take the form of Latin couplets which could be readily impressed upon the pupil's memory. Such *statuta vel precepta scolarium* seem

95

to have been especially popular in the later fifteenth century in those city schools of Germany whose importance has been so clearly brought out by recent historians of secondary education. Wandering often from town to town, like the roving scholars of an earlier age, these German boys had good need to observe the moral maxims thus purveyed. The beginning of wisdom was to remember God and obey the master, but the student had also to watch his behavior in church and lift up his voice in the choir — compulsory attendance at church and singing in the choir being a regular feature of these schools — keep his books clean, and pay his school bills promptly. Face and hands should be washed in the morning, but the baths should not be visited without permission, nor should boys run on the ice or throw snowballs. Sunday was the day for play, but this could be only in the churchyard, where boys must be careful not to play with dice or break stones from the wall or throw anything over the church. And whether at play or at home, Latin should always be spoken.

More systematic is a manual of the fifteenth century preserved in a manuscript of the Bibliothèque Nationale at Paris.[1] " Since by reason of imbecility youths cannot advance to a knowledge of the Latin tongue by theory alone," the author has for their assistance prepared a set of forms which contain the expressions most frequently employed by clerks. Beginning with the courtesies of school life, for obedience and due reverence for the master are the beginning of wisdom, the boy learns how to greet his master and to take leave, how to excuse himself for wrong-doing, how to invite the master to dine or sup with his parents — there are half a dozen forms for this! He is also taught how to give proper answers to those who seek to test his knowledge, " that he may not appear an idiot in the sight of his parents." " If the master asks, 'Where have you been so long?'" he

[1] MS. Lat. n. a. 619, ff. 28–35.

must be ready, not only to plead the inevitable headache or failure to wake up, but also to express the causes of delay well known to any village boy. He had to look after the house or feed the cattle or water the horse; he was detained by a wedding, by picking grapes, or making out bills, or — for these were German boys — by helping with the brew, fetching beer, or serving drink to guests.

In school after the " spiritual refection " of the morning singing-lesson comes refection of the body, which is placed after study hours because " the imaginative virtue is generally impeded in those who are freshly sated." In their talk at luncheon or on the playground " clerks are apt to fall from the Latin idiom into the mother tongue," and for him who speaks German the discretion of the master has invented a dunce's symbol called an ass, which the holder tries hard to pass on to another. " Wer wel ein Griffel kouffe[n] ? " " Ich wel ein Griffel kouffen." " Tecum sit asinus." " Ach,

quam falsus es tu!" Sometimes the
victim offers to meet his deceiver after
vespers, with the usual schoolboy brag on
both sides. As it is forbidden to come to
blows in school, the boys are taught to
work off their enmities and formulate
their complaints in Latin dialogue. "You
were outside the town after dark. You
played with laymen Sunday. You went
swimming Monday. You stayed away
from matins. You slept through mass."
"Reverend master, he has soiled my book,
he shouts after me wherever I go, he calls
me names." Besides the formal disputations the scholars discuss such
current events as a street fight, a cousin's
wedding, the coming war with the duke
of Saxony, or the means of getting to
Erfurt, whither one of them is going when
he is sixteen to study at the university.
The great ordeal of the day was the master's quiz on Latin grammar, when every
one was questioned in turn (*auditio cir-
culi*). The pupils rehearse their declen-
sions and conjugations and the idle begin

to tremble as the hour draws near. There is some hope that the master may not come. "He has guests." "But they will leave in time." "He may go to the baths." "But it is not yet a whole week since he was there last." "There he comes. Name the wolf, and he forthwith appears." Finally the shaky scholar falls back on his only hope, a place near one who promises to prompt him.

"When the recitation is over and the lesson given out, rejoicing begins among the youth at the approach of the hour for going home," and they indulge in much idle talk "which is here omitted, lest it furnish the means of offending." Joy is, however, tempered by the contest which precedes dismissal, " a serious and furious disputation for the *palmiterium*," until one secures the prize and another has the *asinus* to keep till next day.

After school the boys go to play in the churchyard, the sports mentioned being hoops, marbles (apparently), ball (during Lent), and a kind of counting

game. The author distinguishes hoops
for throwing and for rolling, spheres of
wood and of stone, but the subject soon
becomes too deep for his Latin, and in the
midst of this topic the treatise comes to
an abrupt conclusion.

In some of its forms the student
manual touches on territory already oc-
cupied by another type of mediaeval
handbook, the manual of manners, which
under such titles as " The Book of Ur-
banity," " The Courtesies of the Table,"
etc., enjoyed much popularity from the
thirteenth century onward. Such manuals
have, however, none of the polish of
Castiglione's *Courtier* or the elaborate-
ness of the modern book of etiquette.
Those who have not mastered the use of
knife and fork have little use for the finer
points of social intercourse, and the read-
ers of the mediaeval manuals were still
at their a b c's in the matter of behavior.
Wash your hands in the morning and,
if you have time, your face; use your
napkin and handkerchief; eat with three

fingers, and don't gorge; don't be boisterous or quarrelsome at table; don't stare at your neighbor or his plate; don't criticise the food; don't pick your teeth with your knife — such, with others still more elementary, are the maxims which meet us in this period, in Latin and French, in English, German, and Italian, but regularly in verse. Now and then there is a further touch of the age: scrape bones with your knife but don't gnaw them; when you have done with them, put them in a bowl or on the floor!

If the correspondence of mediaeval students were preserved for us in casual and unaffected detail, nothing could give a more vivid picture of university conditions. Unfortunately in some respects for us, the Middle Ages were a period of forms and types in letter-writing as in other things; and for most men the writing of a letter was less an expression of individual feeling and experience than it was the laborious copying of a letter of some one else, altered where necessary to suit the new conditions. And if something fresh or individual was produced, there was small chance of preserving it, since it was on that account all the less likely to be useful to a future letter-writer — " so careful of the type, so careless of the single " letter, history seems. The result is that the hundreds of student letters which have reached us in the manuscripts of the Middle Ages have come down through the medium of collections of forms or complete letter-writers, shorn of most of their individuality but for that very reason reflecting the more faithfully the fundamental and universal phases of university life.

By far the largest element in the correspondence of mediaeval students consists of requests for money; " a student's first song is a demand for money," says a weary father in an Italian letter-writer, " and there will never be a letter which does not ask for cash." How to secure this fundamental necessity of student life was doubtless one of the most important problems that confronted the mediaeval scholar, and many were the models which the rhetoricians placed before him in proof of the practical advantages of their art. The letters are generally addressed to parents, sometimes to brothers, uncles, or ecclesiastical patrons; a much copied exercise contained twenty-two different methods of approaching an archdeacon on this ever-delicate subject. Commonly the student announces that he is at such and such a centre of learning, well and happy but in desperate need of money for books and other necessary expenses. Here is a specimen from Oxford, somewhat more individual than the average and written in uncommonly bad Latin:

" B. to his venerable master A., greeting. This is to inform you that I am studying at Oxford with the greatest diligence, but the matter of money stands greatly in the way of my promotion, as it is now two months since I spent the last of what you sent me. The city is expensive and makes many demands; I have to rent lodgings, buy necessaries, and provide for many other things which I cannot now specify. Wherefore I respectfully beg your paternity that by the promptings of divine pity you may assist me, so that I may be able to complete what I have well begun. For you must know that without Ceres and Bacchus Apollo grows cold."

If the father was close-fisted, there were special reasons to be urged: the town was dear — as university towns always are! — the price of living was exceptionally high owing to a hard winter, a siege, a failure of crops, or an unusual number of scholars; the last messenger had been robbed or had absconded with the money; the son could borrow no more of his fellows or of the Jews; and so on. The student's woes are depicted in moving language, with many appeals to paternal vanity and affection. At Bologna we hear of the terrible mud through which the youth must beg his way from door to door, crying, " O good masters," and coming home empty-handed. In an Austrian formulary a scholar writes from the lowest depths of prison, where the bread is hard and moldy, the drink water mixed with tears, the darkness so dense that it can actually be felt. Another lies on straw with no covering, goes without shoes or shirt, and eats he will not say what — a tale designed to be addressed to a sister and to bring in response a hundred *sous tournois,* two pairs of sheets, and ten ells of fine cloth, all sent without her husband's knowledge. " We have made little glosses, we owe money," is the terse summary of two students at Chartres.

To such requests the proper answer was, of course, an affectionate letter, commending the young man's industry and studious habits and remitting the desired amount. Sometimes the student is cautioned to moderate his expenses — he might have got on longer with what he had, he should remember the needs of his sisters, he ought to be supporting his parents instead of trying to extort money from them, etc. One father — who quotes Horace! — excuses himself because of the failure of his vineyards. It often happened, too, that the father or uncle has heard bad reports of the student, who must then be prepared to deny indignantly all such aspersions as the unfounded fabrications of his enemies. Here is an example of paternal reproof taken from an interesting collection relating to Franche-Comté:

" To his son G. residing at Orleans P. of Besançon sends greetings with paternal zeal. It is written, ' He also that is slothful in his work is brother to him that is a great waster.' I have recently discovered that you live dissolutely and slothfully, preferring license to restraint and play to work and strumming a guitar while the others are at their studies, whence it happens that you have read but one volume of law while your more industrious companions have read several.

107

Wherefore I have decided to exhort you herewith to repent utterly of your dissolute and careless ways, that you may no longer be called a waster and your shame may be turned to good repute."

In the models of Ponce de Provence we find a teacher writing to a student's father that while the young man is doing well in his studies, he is just a trifle wild and would be helped by judicious admonition. Naturally the master does not wish it known that the information came through him, so the father writes his son:

"I have learned — not from your master, although he ought not to hide such things from me, but from a certain trustworthy source — that you do not study in your room or act in the schools as a good student should, but play and wander about, disobedient to your master and indulging in sport and in certain other dishonorable practices which I do not now care to explain by letter." Then follow the customary exhortations to reform.

Two boys at Orleans thus describe their arrival at this centre of learning:

" To their dear and respected parents M. Martre, knight, and M. his wife, M. and S. their sons send greeting and filial obedience. This is to inform you that, by divine mercy, we are living in good health in the city of Orleans and are devoting ourselves wholly to study, mindful of the words of Cato, ' To know anything is praiseworthy.' We occupy a good dwelling, next door but one to the schools and market-place, so that we can go to school every day without wetting our feet. We have also good companions in the house with us, well advanced in their studies and of excellent habits — an advantage which we well appreciate, for as the Psalmist says, ' With an upright man thou wilt show thyself upright.' "

Such youths were slow to quit academic life. Again and again they ask permission to have their term of study extended; war might break out, parents or brothers die, an inheritance have to be divided,

but the student pleads always for delay.
He desires to " serve longer in the camp
of Pallas "; in any event he cannot leave
before Easter, as his masters have just
begun important courses of lectures. A
scholar is called home from Siena to
marry a lady of many attractions; he answers that he deems it foolish to desert
the cause of learning for the sake of a
woman, " for one may always get a wife,
but science once lost can never be recov-
ered."

The time to leave, however, must come
at last, and then the great problem is
money for the expenses of commencement, or, as it was then called, inception.
Thus a student at Paris asks a friend to
explain to his father, " since the simplicity
of the lay mind does not understand such
things," how at length after much study
nothing but lack of money for the inception banquet stands in the way of his
graduation. From Orleans D. Boterel
writes to his dear relatives at Tours that
he is laboring over his last volume of law

and on its completion will be able to pass to his licentiate provided they send him a hundred *livres* for the necessary expenses. An account of the inception at Bologna was quoted in the preceding chapter.[1]

Unlike the student letters, which range over the whole of the later Middle Ages, mediaeval student poetry, or rather the best of it, is limited to a comparatively short period comprised roughly within the years 1125 and 1225, and is closely connected with the classical phase of the twelfth-century renaissance. It is largely the work of the wandering clerks of the period — students, ex-students, professors even — moving from town to town in search of learning and still more of adventure, nominally clerks but leading often very unclerical lives. " Far from their homes," says Symonds, " without responsibilities, light of purse and light of heart, careless and pleasure-seeking, they

---

[1] Supra, p. 67.

ran a free, disreputable course." " They
are wont," writes a monk of the twelfth
century, " to roam about the world and
visit all its cities, till much learning makes
them mad; for in Paris they seek liberal
arts, in Orleans classics, at Salerno medicine, at Toledo magic, but nowhere manners and morals." Their chief habitat,
however, was northern France, the center
of the new literary renaissance.

Possibly from some obscure allusion to
Goliath the Philistine, these wandering
clerks took the name Goliardi and their
verse is generally known as Goliardic poetry. This literature is for the most
part anonymous, though recent research
has individualized certain writers of the
group, notably a Master Hugh, canon of
Orleans, ca. 1142, styled the Primate, and
the so-called Archpoet. The Primate,
mordant, diabolically clever, thoroughly
disreputable, became famous for generations as " an admirable improviser, who if
he had but turned his heart to the love of
God would have had a great place in di-

vine letters and have proved most useful
to God's church." The Archpoet is found
chiefly in Italy from 1161 to 1165, going
" on his own " in spring and summer but
when autumn comes on turning to beg
shirt and cloak from his patron, the arch-
bishop of Cologne. Ordered to compose
an epic for the emperor in a week, he re-
plies he cannot write on an empty stomach
— the quality of his verse depends on the
quality of his wine:

Tales versus facio quale vinum bibo.

Good wine he must at times have found,
for he composed the masterpiece of the
whole school, the Confession of a Goliard,
that unforgettable description of the
burning temptations of Pavia which contains the famous glorification of the joys
of the tavern:

> In the public house to die
>   Is my resolution;
> Let wine to my lips be nigh
>   At life's dissolution;

That will make the angels cry,
   With glad elocution,
" Grant this toper, God on high,
   Grace and absolution! "

Though written in Latin, the Goliardic
verse has abandoned the ancient metrical
system for the rhyme and accent of modern poetry, but even the best of modern
versions, such as those of John Addington
Symonds, from which I am quoting, fail
to render the swing, the lilt, the rhyth-
mical flow of the original. Its authors
are familiar with classical mythology and
especially with the writings of Ovid,
whose precepts, copied even in severe
Cluny, were freely followed. Most of
all is this poetry classical in its frankly
pagan view of life. Its gods are Venus
and Bacchus, also Decius, the god of dice.
Love and wine and spring, life on the
open road and under the blue sky, these
are the common subjects; the spirit is
that of an intense delight in the world that
is, a joy in mere living, such as one finds

in the Greek and Roman poets or in that sonorous song of a later age which the academic world still cherishes,

Gaudeamus igitur iuvenes dum sumus.

In general the Goliardic poetry is of an impersonal sort, giving us few details from any particular place, but reflecting the gayer, more jovial, less reputable side of the life of mediaeval clerks. The worshipful order of vagrants is described, open to men of every condition and every clime, with its rules which are no rules, late-risers, gamesters, roysterers, proud that none of its members has more than one coat to his back, begging their way from town to town with requests for money which sound like students' letters in verse:

I, a wandering scholar lad,
Born for toil and sadness,
Oftentimes am driven by
Poverty to madness.

115

THE RISE OF UNIVERSITIES

Literature and knowledge I
  Fain would still be earning,
Were it not that want of pelf
  Makes me cease from learning.

These torn clothes·that cover me
  Are too thin and rotten;
Oft I have to suffer cold,
  By the warmth forgotten.

Scarce I can attend at church,
  Sing God's praises duly;
Mass and vespers both I miss,
  Though I love them truly.

Oh, thou pride of N——,
  By thy worth I pray thee
Give the suppliant help in need,
  Heaven will sure repay thee.

Take a mind unto thee now
  Like unto St. Martin;
Clothe the pilgrim's nakedness,
  Wish him well at parting.

So may God translate your soul
  Into peace eternal,
And the bliss of saints be yours
  In His realm supernal.

THE MEDIAEVAL STUDENT

The brethren greet each other at wayside
taverns with songs like this:

> We in our wandering,
> Blithesome and squandering,
>   Tara, tantara, teino!
>
> Eat to satiety,
> Drink with propriety;
>   Tara, tantara, teino!
>
> Laugh till our sides we split,
> Rags on our hides we fit;
>   Tara, tantara, teino!
>
> Jesting eternally,
> Quaffing infernally:
>   Tara, tantara, teino!
>   etc.

The assembled topers are described in
another poem:

> Some are gaming, some are drinking,
> Some are living without thinking;
> And of those who make the racket,
> Some are stripped of coat and jacket;
> Some get clothes of finer feather,
> Some are cleaned out altogether;
> No one there dreads death's invasion,
> But all drink in emulation.

drink heavily

Then they sacrilegiously drink once for all prisoners and captives, three times for the living, a fourth time for the whole body of Christians, a fifth for those departed in the faith, and so on to the thirteenth for those who travel by land or water, and a final and unlimited potation for king and Pope. Such poetry is plainly the expression of a ' wet ' age.

Often bibulous and erotic, the Goliardic verse contains a large amount of parody and satire. Appealing to a public familiar with scripture and liturgy, its authors parody anything — the Bible, hymns to the Virgin, the canon of the mass, as in the " Drinkers' Mass " and the " Office for Gamblers." One of the best-known pieces is a satire on the Papacy under the caption of " The Gospel according to Mark-s of silver." This is only one of many bitter attacks on Rome, while the pride, hardness, and greed of the higher clergy are portrayed in " Golias the Bishop." The point of view in general is that of the lower clergy, especially

118

the looser, wandering, undisciplined element which frequented the schools and the roads, the *jongleurs* of the clerical world, familiar subjects of ecclesiastical legislation since the ninth century.

Poetry of this sort is so contrary to conventional conceptions of the Middle Ages that some writers have denied its mediaeval character. " It is," says one, " mediaeval only in the chronological sense," while others find in it close affinities with the spirit of the Renaissance or of the Reformation. It would be more consonant with the spirit of history to enlarge our ideas of the Middle Ages so as to correspond to the facts of mediaeval life. The Goliardi were neither humanists before the Renaissance nor reformers before the Reformation; they were simply men of the Middle Ages who wrote for their own time. If the writings of these northern and chiefly French clerks seem to anticipate the Italian Renaissance, it may be that the Renaissance began earlier and was less specifically Italian than has been supposed. If the authors are more secular, even more earthy, than we should expect clerks to be, we must learn to expect something different. In lyric poetry, as in the epic and the drama, we are now learning more of the close interpenetration of the lay and ecclesiastical worlds, no longer separated by the air-tight partitions which the imagination of a later day interposed. And whether their spirit was lay or ecclesiastical, the Goliardi were certainly human; they saw and felt life keenly, and they wrote of what they knew.

It is time to redress the balance with a word about a less obtrusive element, the good student. "The life of the virtuous student," says Dean Rashdall, "has no annals," [1] and in all ages he has been less conspicuous than his more dashing fellows. Thus the ideal scholar of the sermons is a bit colorless but obedient, respectful, eager to learn, assiduous at lectures, and bold in debate, pondering his

---

[1] *Universities,* II, p. 692.

lessons even during his evening prom-
enades by the river. The ideal student of
the manuals is he who practices their precepts. The typical student of the letters
has already described himself as devoted
wholly to study, though somewhat short
of money. The good student of the poems
— there is no such person! Student
poetry was " not all bacchic or erotic or
profane," [1] but much of it was, and we
must not look here for the more serious
side of academic life. Jean de Hauteville's account of the poor and industrious
scholar is representative of a large class of
students but not of a large body of poetry.
The good student's occupations are best
reflected in the course of study, his assi-
duity best seen in his note-books and disputations. The documents which concern
the educational side of the university are
also a source for student life! It has been
observed that the alumni reunions of our
own day are often more prolific in rec-
ollections of student escapades than of

[1] *Ib.*, II, p. 686, note.

121

the daily performance of the allotted task. The studious lad of today never breaks into the headlines as such, and no one has seen fit to produce a play or a film " featuring the good student." Yet everyone familiar with contemporary universities knows that the serious student exists in large numbers, and it has been shown conclusively that the distinction he there achieves reflects itself in his later life. So it was in the Middle Ages. The law students of Bologna insisted on their money's worth of teaching from their professors. The examinations described by Robert de Sorbon required serious preparation. Not only was the vocational motive a strong incentive to study in the mediaeval university, but there was much enthusiasm for knowledge and much discussion of intellectual subjects. The greater universities, at least, were intellectually very much alive, with something of that ' religion of learning ' which had earlier called Abelard's pupils into the wilderness, there to build themselves huts that they might feed upon his words. The books of the age were in large measure written by its professors, and the students had the advantage of seeing them in the making and thus drinking of learning at its fountain-head. Then as now, the moral quality of a university depended on the intensity and seriousness of its intellectual life.

If we consider the body of student literature as a whole, its most striking, and its most disappointing, characteristic is its lack of individuality. The *Manuale Scholarium* is written for the use of all scholars who propose to attend universities of students. The letters are made as general as possible in order to fit the need of any student who wants money, clothes, or books. Even the poems, where we have some right to expect personal expression of feeling, have the generic character of most mediaeval poetry; they are for the most part the voice of a class, not of individuals.

At the same time it must be remembered that this characteristic of the student productions, if it robs them of something of their interest, increases their historical value. The historian deals with the general rather than the particular, and his knowledge must be built up by a painful collection and comparison of individual facts, which are often too few or too unlike to admit of sound generalization. In the case of these student records, however, that labor has already been performed for him; in the form in which they come down to us they have lost, at the hands of the students themselves, what is local and peculiar and exceptional, and have become, what in view of the nature of our information no historian could hope to make them, the generalized experience of centuries of student life.

It is this broadly human quality that gives the productions of the mediaeval student a special interest for the world of today. In substance, though not in form, many of them are almost as representative of modern Harvard or Yale as of mediaeval Oxford or Paris. The Latin dialogue and disputation, the mud of Bologna, and the money-changers of the Grand-Pont, belong plainly in the Middle Ages and not in our time; but money and clothing, rooms, teachers, and books, good cheer and good fellowship, have been subjects of interest at all times and all places. A professor of history once said that the greatest difficulty of historical teaching lay in convincing pupils that the events of the past did not all happen in the moon. The Middle Ages are very far away, farther from us in some respects than is classical antiquity, and it is very hard to realize that men and women, then and now, are after all much the same human beings. We need constantly to be reminded that the fundamental factors in man's development remain much the same from age to age and must so remain as long as human nature and physical environment continue what they have been. In his relations to life and learning the mediaeval student resembled his modern successor far more than is often supposed. If his environment was different, his problems were much the same; if his morals were perhaps worse, his ambition was as active, his rivalries as intense, his desire for learning quite as keen. And for him as for us, intellectual achievement meant membership in that city of letters not made with hands, " the ancient and universal company of scholars."

BIBLIOGRAPHICAL NOTE

I

The standard work on mediaeval universities is Hastings Rashdall, *The Universities of Europe in the Middle Ages* (Oxford, 1895; new edition in preparation), to which my indebtedness will be apparent throughout. The later literature can be most easily found in L. J. Paetow, *Guide to the Study of Mediaeval History* (Berkeley, 1917). Important materials are conveniently accessible in translation in D. C. Munro, *The Mediaeval Student* (Philadelphia, 1895); and A. O. Norton, *Readings in the History of Education: Mediaeval Universities* (Cambridge, Mass., 1909). Bologna now has a cartulary and a special series of *Studî e Memorie* (both since 1907); while the municipal history of the early period has been studied by A. Hessel, *Geschichte der Stadt Bologna von 1116 bis 1280* (Berlin, 1910). Light has recently been thrown on Salerno by the studies of Giacosa and Sudhoff and the dissertations of Sudhoff's pupils; its most popular product, *The School of Salernum*, can be read

127

in the quaint English version of Sir John Harrington, recently reprinted (London, 1922) with a good note by F. H. Garrison and a less valuable preface by Francis R. Packard. Paris still lacks a modern historian; Mullinger is still the standard work on Cambridge; while Oxford can best be studied in Rashdall, supplemented, as in the case of Cambridge, by the histories of the several colleges.

II

The most useful general work on the content of mediaeval learning is Henry Osborn Taylor, *The Mediaeval Mind* (third edition, New York, 1919). This may be supplemented by R. L. Poole, *Illustrations of the History of Mediaeval Thought and Learning* (second edition, London, 1920); M. Grabmann, *Geschichte der scholastischen Methode* (Freiburg, 1909–11); Sir J. E. Sandys, *History of Classical Scholarship*, I (third edition, Cambridge, 1921); Lynn Thorndike, *History of Magic and Experimental Science* (New York, 1923); Pierre Duhem, *Le système du monde de Platon à Copernic*, II–V (Paris, 1914–17); Charles H. Haskins, *Studies in the History of Mediaeval Science* (in press, Harvard University Press); the standard histories of philosophy, mathematics, law,

and medicine; and the more special literature
in Paetow's *Guide*, including his own study of
the *Arts Course* (Urbana, 1910) and his edition of the *Battle of the Seven Arts* (Berkeley,
1914). For a sample of Abelard's *Sic et Non*,
see Norton, *Readings*, pp. 20–25. Abelard's
method can be followed further in the logical
writings edited for the first time by B. Geyer
in Baeumker's *Beiträge zur Geschichte der
Philosophie des Mittalalters*, XXI (Münster,
1919 ff.). The best account of the class-rooms
of a mediaeval university is F. Cavazza, *Le
scuole dell' antico studio bolognese* (Milan,
1896). Robert de Sorbon's *De conscientia* is
edited by Chambon (Paris, 1903).

III

Brief sketches of student life will be found
in the last chapter of Rashdall and in the little
volume of R. S. Rait, *Life in the Mediaeval
University* (Cambridge, 1912). In the text
I have drawn freely from an article of my own
on student letters (*American Historical Re-
view*, III, pp. 203–229) and from one on the
Paris sermons (*ib.*, X, pp. 1–27). John of
Garlande's *Dictionary* will be found most conveniently in T. Wright, *A Volume of Vocabu-
laries* (London, 1882), pp. 120–138; he also

wrote a *Morale Scolarium* of which Paetow is preparing an edition. The *Manuale Scholarium* has been translated and annotated by R. F. Seybolt (Harvard University Press, 1921). *Statuta vel Precepta Scolarium* have been edited by M. Weingart (Metten, 1894) and by P. Bahlmann in *Mitteilungen der Gesellschaft für deutsche Erziehungs- und Schulgeschichte,* III, pp. 129–145 (1893). The latest discussion of mediaeval manuals of manners is by S. Glixelli, in *Romania,* XLVII, pp. 1–40 (1921). The best single collection of Goliardic verse is J. A. Schmeller, *Carmina Burana* (Breslau, 1894); the best translations are those of J. A. Symonds, *Wine, Women, and Song.* Two poets have since been individualized, the Primate by Léopold Delisle and W. Meyer, the Archpoet by B. Schmeidler and M. Manitius. For an introduction to the vast literature of Goliardic poetry, see Paetow's *Guide,* pp. 449 f.; P. S. Allen, in *Modern Philology,* V, VI; and H. Süssmilch, *Lateinische Vagantenpoesie* (Leipzig, 1917). On the origin of the word ' Goliardi,' see James Westfall Thompson, in the *Studies in Philology,* published by the University of North Carolina, XX, pp. 83–98 (1923).

INDEX

INDEX

132

INDEX

INDEX